MW00423792

BREASTFEEDING

is a

BITCH

But we lovingly do it anyway

BY CASSI CLARK

Printed in the United States of America

First Printing, 2014

ISBN 978-1-6319225-5-8
www.cassiclark.com
www.breastfeedingisabitch.com

Austin
April 2015

The Caveats and Characters

This book is not intended for diagnosis, but for entertainment and commiseration. In it, I tell my own story of agonizing, discouraging and sometimes blissful breastfeeding. I have also included stories told to me by many generous, loving mommas. Their names have been changed or left out to protect the innocent and their babies. In most cases, I used names of saints or names that mean saint because any woman who embarks on a life of motherhood, and the resultant sacrifice of mind, body and heart, is a saint. Below is a guide to who's who.

THE SAINTS

St. Monica is the patron saint of mothers and suffered over her son, as did a lovely woman I met through a local Denver momma support store. She warmly invited me, and other women she'd just met to her play dates for new moms, and unbeknownst to her, saved me from some pretty scary loneliness and baby blues.

My *Friend with Twins* has raised four smart, talented children, now young adults. We met through a mutual friend (who loved breastfeeding) and bonded over skiing here in Colorado. She is my exemplar of being her own wonderful person while retaining her love of being a mom – an identity adjustment that took me a while to embrace.

Fiachra is an Irish female name meaning Irish Saint, and this woman is both Irish and a saint. The mother of a friend, she has always taken care of my family as if we were her own. She is open and generous with her life and heart. She is the kind of person I am working to be. Fiachra raised her children in Eastern Virginia.

My oldest cousin in New Hampshire has always been a role model for me. When I was ten-years-old, she held for me that cool-older-kid allure. She still holds that cool allure, but now it is because she is a dynamo. She is smart, strong, kind and generous. She had a lovely home birth (of which I am in awe) with midwives; only to be abandoned when she gave up on breastfeeding after ample bouts of mastitis. I named her *Jane* after Saint Jane of Valois because they both suffered illness.

Like her namesake, my Saint *Adele* is first a wife and mother. Though I have not met this woman in person – she is the wife of one of The Best Husband Ever's coworkers, and lives in New Mexico – she is known as a great mom and wife. (I did meet her husband, who spoke so lovingly about her.) She and I bonded over tongue-tied babies, and she generously shared deeply about her experiences.

My *Cousin in Scotland* gave me great perspective with her stories on transitioning to solid foods, and the advice given "over the pond." She is also an example of someone for whom breastfeeding came easy, and since I love her, I do not begrudge her. It's good to know people who had it easy, so the rest of us know what's abnormal and go get help.

Saint Elizabeth Ann Seton was a mother and an educator, and devoted her life to children. My **Saint Elizabeth** is a godly woman devoted to her family and helping others. Like so many of us, she did not fully grasp what she was in for, but gracefully rose to the challenge. Elizabeth and I met being ski bums in Wyoming; she and her family now live in Utah.

My **RN Friend** is the spunky, full-of-life kind of mom we all need to know. She is full of humor and encouragement that makes even the toughest times seem like nothing more than fodder for great stories later. She's the kind of woman that gives moms a good name and makes me want to be part of the club. She lives in Oregon. Go Ducks!

Saeran is Welsh name meaning saint, she and her husband were saints in helping The Best Husband Ever and I prepare for everything baby. They did the research in raising their own beautiful daughter, and passed on the best pieces of advice and hand-me-downs. Without them we would have been lost.

They say nothing prepares you for having a baby, but having a baby. And, nothing prepares you for having a baby and getting pneumonia, but damn, if you can get through that you can do anything! My **PA friend** is a smart, strong, resilient woman who is unstoppable. We should all be so lucky to have her endurance.

Riona means saint, and like her name indicates, she is amazing. Riona defends the put-upon, cares for everyone in her family, volunteers for arts and culture, and is genuinely the nicest person I know. Her positivity and new mom commiseration have helped me find confidence in my own role of mom.

Along the journey of this book, I sometimes met people who were extraordinarily excited about this project. One such person was a *friend's cousin* who told me about her Impending Sense of Doom (See Screaming at the Breast). Her enthusiasm and excitement to share; and the enthusiasm of those like her; made this book possible, and rewarding.

They (correctly) say it takes a village to raise a family. Some people, like me, get adopted into said villages, while others create those amazing villages. *Phiala*, meaning saint, not only adopted me into her village, but champions mommy-hood so that we might all have villages. Also in my village are my naturopath, a professor from my Master's program, women in our baby training class, all the women in my family and my friends' families, my fellow writer's circle peeps and their spouses, and a very helpful neighbor who passed along encouragement and baby containment devices.

CONTENTS

Introduction

Breastfeeding is a bitch. Don't let that bullshit line "women have been doing it for millennia" fool you. Successfully breastfeeding takes courage, resilience, patience, and support, and it always has. If your partner or support group hasn't piled on the accolades for your heroism, then let them know you will expect oohs and ahs when you make it through the first two to three months (no matter how you got there) and your baby is happy and healthy – because you are awesome.

"Breastfeeding is being championed. Yay!" We cheer on social media, and around our female friends with feminist pride. But at three a.m. you may be cudgeling yourself with, "Oh, dear god, what have we done." Intellectually, we all know it's better for our babies, and instinctually, many of us want to do it. But our pregnant daydreaming does little to prepare us for the pain, frustration, self-judgment, and fear that we may experience by choosing to breastfeed.

In case you haven't heard, let me tell you now, babies *do not* come out knowing how to breastfeed. It is nothing like TV, where the too-large-to-be-a-newborn nuzzles into his momma's normal-sized breast and suckles in perfect bliss while she smiles and coos above. Newborn babies are small creatures with very small mouths, and for the first few days, weeks (and sometimes months), most of us nursing moms have sensitive nipples on boobs the size of our newborn's head. Your cousin with the breastfeeding stories approximating angels and rainbows is either lying, or one of the lucky ones (don't worry, her troubles likely will appear elsewhere, like sleep issues).

For a happy few, the initial pain of having a baby latch onto the most sensitive nerve endings on our bodies only lasts a week. But it is a wild week, fueled by hormones that make your craziest pregnancy-days look tame; anxiety about everything; and constant concern about whether or not your baby is latched properly, eating enough, and gaining weight.

For the rest of us, breastfeeding is filled with concerns about not enough milk, or extreme engorgement pain, vasospasm of the nipple, tongue-tie, mastitis, improper mouth shape, baby not latching, picky eaters, screaming at the breast, sleeping on the breast – the list goes on.

This is my story, but not just my story. It also is the story of over 25 friends, family members and acquaintances. These saints generously answered my Facebook and email call with heartfelt tales of hard times, funny anecdotes, and even some angel and rainbow moments. These are our stories of the amazing, and amazingly hard time, that is feeding an infant. Our stories are partly funny, partly irreverent, way too graphic, and totally awesome, all at once. They cover the gamut of breastfeeding experiences from agony to sainthood, and from torment to bliss.

And, they are every mother's story, regardless of how you fed your baby.

Hopefully, our tales will diminish your feelings of isolation, so that you can have as much sweet feeding time as you and your baby want.

Hang in there, girl! Breastfeeding is a bitch, but we lovingly do it anyway.

CHAPTER 1

Getting To Baby

When I was a teenager I had my first, and really only, pregnancy dream. Looking back, I am sure the dream had some deep meaning, like some aspect of myself was growing and developing, or was a representation of the birth of a new idea, direction, or goal. But at the time, it scared the hell out of me. I didn't want to have a kid. I feared being a mom, being responsible for another human being. I convinced myself that I would be a terrible mom and screw over any children I had, with both my nature and my nurture.

I stuck with this idea until I was thirty, and got attached to the man who would eventually become The Best Husband Ever. But, before we got there, we had to get to know each other.

At four months of dating, he decided to see how much of the stuff I spouted about my life goals was really true. It was the make-it-or-break-it date. (Not sure how I didn't break it.) He wanted to know if I was worth the energy. So, he started digging through my emotional BS until he hit my well-fortified emotional wall. Over martinis (both of us dressed all cute like you do when you're dating), he asked me question after question, which I answered through giggles and streaming tears. He didn't buy most of my answers; he would reject and ask again. Eventually, we both got down to the real me, and he decided I was worth his energy. In that conversation, he made me feel safe, both in a future with him and with becoming a parent. Not having a kid was a deal breaker for him, so by the time we got married I had agreed. To one.

Of course, it took me a while to be emotionally and physically "ready." We had planned to be one of those couples that got pregnant on purpose at the perfect time. We argued over whether we wanted another Pisces like me (not his first choice), or another Leo like him (not my first choice). In the end, the perfect time was precipitated by a mix of being off birth control for medical reasons, taking a trip to LA, and enjoying some gin on St. Paddy's Day – about six months before we'd planned.

I should tell you now that I was not a glowing, happy pregnant lady. I hated being pregnant. My hair got all stringy; my skin broke out; I was exhausted; and I was uncomfortable in my own skin. To top it off, I gained forty pounds despite regularly exercising and not overeating. Turns out, like my mom, I swell.

But I survived. I saved The Best Husband Ever from my emotional freak-outs and tirades by making him go out and socialize with our friends regardless of what he actually wanted to do. We carved out a little place in our apartment for the baby (affectionately named the Baby Cave), and took classes to learn how to care for an infant – and how to get it out of me.

When the baby stayed breech, we did all the crazy gymnastics prescribed by oldwives tales, tried acupuncture and worked some Chinese incense magic[1]. With a week left to go, we gave up on turning the baby and found a doctor who would deliver him vaginally. It was stressful having to fire the OB that had gotten us to thirty-eight weeks, but I refused to have surgery just because she didn't know how to deliver a breech baby. Like a shock victim holding an electric wire, I latched onto having a vaginal birth and breastfeeding my baby. I just couldn't let it go.

Labor was, as the word implies, really hard work. The first twelve hours were tolerable in that go-shopping-and-eat-out-at-a-restaurant way that our birthing class teacher filled us with fantasizes of. The next part was not so awesome. After three or four hours of the vomit-and-stick-close-to-the-toilet labor that I most definitely did not fantasize about, I promptly abandoned at least half of what we'd learned in that natural child-birth class and called for an epidural. The reward was seven or eight hours of medically induced, blissful excitement[2]. The last part resembled a Pinterest workout. After two hours of squats (holding onto the back of the bed), we had a healthy, very blond, baby boy, whom I greeted with "Holy Shit." I was shocked that this beautiful creature came out of me, and couldn't believe he looked like me rather than a miniature version of the Best Husband Ever.

As we settled into our recovery room and I made close friends

---

1   Moxibustion

2   If you have the chance, ask for a light dose, you can still move around on the bed some and your contractions feel like little baby kicks.

with my icepack, I marveled at how perfect he was, and rested in the knowledge that the hard part was over. Or so I thought. Having a vaginal breech birth was a bitch, but breastfeeding would be a piece of cake, right?

*I didn't know they existed either until my daughter's pediatrician handed me the calling card of a Cathy Clark (lactation consultant) which mentioned breastfeeding classes, and didn't know they took place during pregnancy, not after childbirth, till I called them.

CHAPTER 2

I'm Supposed to Keep This Baby Alive?!

Like so many new parents, The Best Husband Ever and I attended as many baby-training classes as we could stand – but no ✳ breastfeeding classes. (I have no idea why. I'm going to pretend they didn't exist, but they probably did, because our peers claim to have attended some.) In our nothing-to-do-with-feeding classes, we learned "what to expect during labor," which, nothing really can prepare you for, except I assume, doing it. (I have only one kid so far, so I cannot say for sure if going through labor once prepares you for it the second time.) Our childbirth teacher had us practice labor breathing while holding an ice cube in our hands. I can absolutely assure you that birth is nothing like holding an ice cube in your hand for a minute and breathing through the "pain."

We also learned how to keep My Little Milkaholic (then just a little energy sucking, fat making, fetus) safe and SIDS free (apparently the trick is simply not having or using anything, ever because everything is potentially lethal), and how to attach a disposable diaper to a non-moving doll and give it a bath. Imagine our surprise when My Little Milkaholic started crawling and decided diapers were no longer necessary, and were worth fighting to the death over!

In one class, we were told that before we would be allowed to leave the hospital, a nurse would approve our new parenting skills. We had no delusions of preparedness. We were as ready as we could be, and were fortified by the thought of the teachings the nurses in the post-partum recovery room would provide us in the context of our real, moving baby. We were we ready to be taught and to dazzle!

Oh, how we were misled.

My Cousin in Scotland was offered lessons in the hospital on bathing her baby and changing "nappies." Here in America, my saintly Friend With Twins is the only woman I know who got baby-care training from the nurses. They took advantage of the extra time she spent in the hospital after birth, recovering from a bruised bladder. She said this was a "good thing, because I was young (twenty-two), and we were 800 miles from family."

At our hospital there was a checklist, but it was for stuff like vaccines and pediatric check-ups. There was nothing about how to put a giant cloth diaper on a tiny moving target; how to keep a slippery, wet wiggly being above water in the bath; or even lessons on how much torque is actually acceptable to get baby arms into the infinitely cute and tiny clothes that suddenly appear with every mail delivery.

On all the hospital tours we took (three in Denver), each bragged in turn about their lactation consultation services. The hospital where we'd originally planned to have My Little

Milkaholic, even claimed to have trained lactation specialists on every shift. The others, including the hospital where we actually had My Little Milkaholic[3], had nurses with lactation certifications. For a semi-prepared, soon-to-be new mom, this was the magic phrase. I knew breastfeeding could be hard. While most of the stories I heard were distant memories of it being easy (like being able to sleep while the baby fed), from friends and family member's whose babies are in their twenties and thirties, I also had a couple friends whose babies never latched. So, I knew successful breastfeeding was not certain. I imagined it would take my angel a few tries to get it. I would show him how to open his mouth, as an aunt of mine had done with her nursling. He would mimic, and then eat to his stomach's content.

It was a nice fantasy. The unfortunate reality of in-hospital lactation help was much like learning to bathe or dress My Little Milkaholic: the help was there, but you had to know you were having problems and ask for it.

When My Little Milkaholic came out, our doula put him on my chest and helped him root around for my nipple while I stared in shock at his existence. She talked about the importance of rooting for his brain development (or something, the memory is a little foggy), and the benefits of colostrum (the weird liquid that comes out before your milk has actually come in).

In the post-partum recovery room, the first nurse showed

---

3   Of the many hospitals in Denver, only one has nurses trained to help deliver breech babies, and is the only hospital at which the only doctor who will still deliver breech babies will work.

"flatten it like a sandwich" said one of the nurse practitioner whom I took Ariana to see for a possible cold. The mucus in her nose was actually me how to squish my boob and shove it in My Little Milkaholic's dried mouth. It seemed a bit violent, but ever a good student, I did as milk that told. She instructed me on the three favored positions: Cradle hold had (arms crossed to hold his head), football hold, and side-lying hold. three Then, she would leave us to our business. After we'd stopped, she over-would return, and ask me if he latched, and how long he'd fed. eating. She never actually watched us feed. I would dutifully answer her questions, having no idea what a real latch was, or if he was getting anything in his belly. He was suckling, and sometimes my boob even stayed in his mouth. That's what breastfeeding was, right?

The second day, we had My Little Milkaholic circumcised, which caused him to sleep all day, skipping meals (which we were told was normal) and crucial nursing practice time. To doubly thwart any further training, like most women, my milk did not come in while I was in the hospital. So, while it seemed like My Little Milkaholic was latching fine, there was really no way (for me) to tell if he was actually eating.

No one asked if he was making obvious swallowing sounds. No one watched a feeding to make sure it was working right. No one seemed to assume we would/were having any problems. And then they sent us home.

The day after we brought My Sweet Little Milkaholic home, we pranced out (as directed) to our pediatrician to show him off. Proud of our accomplishment of having produced a live human, and having proved our superior parenting skills – gleaned from the fact the hospital let us take him home – we delightedly handed My

Little Milkaholic over for cooing and congratulating. The medical assistant weighed him and the Physician's Assistant-Lactation Consultant (PA-LC) did an initial exam.

It's possible they cooed and congratulated, but when the PA-LC announced he'd lost fourteen percent of his body weight (seven percent or less was the standard acceptable amount for U.S. doctors in 2012), I lost my shit. She was worried he was a little dehydrated, but all my hormone-addled brain heard was that I was starving my baby. Thus began the one and only time I was truly the stereotypical, crazy hormonal (although no longer) pregnant woman, stifling weeping and unending tears. (The Best Husband Ever agrees that that was the only crazy time. That is not sarcasm in his voice, he just sounds like that.)

Our PA-LC vacillated between assuring me that My Little Milkaholic was fine, that he was not dying, and worrying about sending us to the hospital in the midst of flu season. In an attempt to rehydrate him, she gave us a two-ounce bottle of formula to feed him there in the office as a stop gap, and assured naïve, hormonal, bawling me that a bit of formula now would only help him breastfeed once my milk came in, and would not make him grow up to be obese. (I'd heard of a study that linked formula to obesity, which later was mostly debunked.)

God has a sick sense of humor. It can take three or four days after birth for a woman's milk to come in. When our hormones are at their worst, causing severe craziness and emotional instability, and when our babies need it the most, our milk isn't there.

After My Little Milkaholic drank enough formula to give him the energy to try breastfeeding again, our PA-LC once again taught me how to squish my breast and jam it into his mouth. To which he responded by screaming. I think I would scream too if someone violently jammed a big ass breast in my mouth, especially given that it is supposed to go to the back of his mouth, which seems a lot like trying to swallow a football whole.

Eventually calmed, if a little dehydrated (all of us), she sent us home, with instructions to get a hospital-grade pump, and start using it immediately to suck my milk into action. She assured me that I would know when it "came in," though at the time I could not even imagine it. So much of this process of having a baby was basically unfathomable to me until it happened.

That evening, after I had successfully pumped four ounces of milk and finally quit crying, we settled into the porter that my doula had promised would help my milk come in, and were discussing how to acquire a cooked steak, also a doula prescription.

And then our pediatrician called.

Now if you ask The Best Husband Ever, she said something like My Little Milkaholic's "sodium is high and I want you to take him to the hospital after dinner to get some fluids. There's no rush; he's fine. It is basically routine for us to send babies to the hospital to get IVs for dehydration because of the lag time between birth and mother's milk coming in."

I, of course, heard, "Your baby is dying. You are unfit to be a parent. You are a failure for not being able to feed your baby." Saying it now, months later, it sounds so dramatic. But that is the beauty of post-partum hormones – intense, crazy-ass emotions. I don't think I have ever cried so hard in my entire life. The Best Husband Ever says he was surprised they didn't have to give me a Quaalude and my own IV for dehydration.

The hardest part of a pediatrician's job must be dealing with parents. This was especially the case for the one on call when we arrived at the hospital. It turns out giving newborn babies an IV for dehydration *is* very common, and because My Little Milkaholic was so lethargic from being dehydrated, he didn't care at all about getting poked with the needle (three times, because they couldn't find a vein). He didn't even cry, the little champ. Or so they tell me. Smartly, the doctor had my mother-in-law take me out of the room to get dinner. Turns out crying gave me an appetite (but then I've never been the woman who loses weight when I get upset or sick). Magically, hours passed as if minutes, and it was way past dinner time.

Once My Little Milkaholic was settled, a nurse from the maternity ward came down to see if she could help get him to latch. With a room full of family, nurses and periodically the doctor; I sat half-naked, alternately squishing and having my boob squished into My Little Milkaholic's mouth. And he screamed. We finally gave up and gave him a bottle of my newly pumped milk, which he guzzled like a frat boy sucking on a beer bong at spring break. The nurse encouraged me to continue trying, but to not work either him or myself to the point of tears.

After four or five hours, we left. My Little Milkaholic was back up to only a five percent loss from his birth weight. The doctor warned us that he would probably have lost that weight gain in the morning when we returned to our pediatrician's, but that was OK.

The next morning, with great dread and a whole lot of Kleenex, we returned to the doctor's office. My Little Milkaholic was up to only four percent weight loss from birth. By a week later he was four ounces above his birth weight, and in the ninetieth percentile for height. And, the doctor said we didn't have to come back for two whole weeks! Apparently, I made buttermilk[4] and My Little Milkaholic loved it. He greedily drank two to four ounces from a bottle every two or three hours. (KellyMom, a breastfeeding and parenting website and Google's favorite search answer at the time for everything baby information, says babies on average take in twenty-five ounces a day. I think My Little Milkaholic was taking in between thirty and forty ounces).

We had survived the craziest three days of my life, and were finally ready to get into a groove. I craved a routine for catharsis, some amount of normalcy I could depend on as I got used to our new life. I pictured sweet nursing time on a regular schedule with cuddling naps between to make up for no longer

---

4   I found out later that not all milk is the same. Some women, like my Friend with Twins and me, make heavy whipping cream while other women make whole, 2% or even skim milk.

sleeping through the night. Such a sweet fantasy.

CHAPTER 3

Latching onto Latching

The fantasy of sweet nursing time was a reality for a few lucky women I talked to before and after I had My Little Milkaholic. I once read a book where these vapid socialites "channeled Kate Hudson" whenever they wanted to look good. It was a terrible book, but I adopted the concept. Throughout my pregnancy and breastfeeding, I channeled every person with good/easy/blissful birth and nursing stories that I could find. I do believe that what we picture or believe will happen, for the most part; the key is to get unstuck from the horror stories we latch onto.

My mother and two best friends told me how they loved breastfeeding because it was so relaxing, and how it was a great bonding experience for them. Unfortunately, channeling their stories didn't work for me; we'll get to that in a minute (or chapter to be more exact). I do however, hold hope for our species in knowing that some women do have it relatively easy (relative being the key word).

A friend whose baby is a week younger than My Little Milkaholic, whom I'll call Saint Riona, told me her nursling latched like a Hungry, Hungry Hippo. "He latched right away," she said. "I have no idea what it felt like because I was in awe that I was holding my very own tiny human." My neighborhood saintly naturopath was lucky that way too. She said her nursling would start sucking anywhere he could find skin. "One time when I was asleep, he latched onto my nose," she said.

Having some pain or problems in the first week is pretty common, and although they can still be "good breastfeeding" stories, it does not mean they are without emotional turmoil. For some women there is a great fear surrounding breastfeeding. It is an unidentified fear, a sinking feeling, an unnamed anxiety. A friend of mine's saintly cousin called this fear her "Impending Sense of Doom." Every single time she nursed any of her three children she would experience this fear. She trained her family to tell her everything was going to be OK and to cheer her on. Once her nursling latched, the fear would go away. I picture her husband and other kids cheering her on, pompoms in hand, every three hours. While the fear part is awful, having a cheering squad every time you feed your baby seems awesome!

A friend's mom, Saint Fiachra (an Irish saint), told me her story:

> I went into motherhood prepared for delivery, but not for what was to happen when the baby was born. They brought her to me right away for her first nursing, but she fell asleep. When she woke up she was not able to latch on. I'd go down to the nursery

and try to nurse her, but it didn't work. The nurses urged bottles, but I wouldn't do it. I was very, very committed to nursing.

When we went home in two days, Twittlebug still hadn't nursed. The hospital staff sent us home with diapers and a six-pack of bottles. I was *soo* terrified. I remember my Dear Husband getting the car while I was wheeled out to the hospital entrance, thinking, 'How can they send me home with this baby – I don't know how to take care of her!' Sheer terror! We had no family to help, no friends nearby because we had only been in Virginia for three years and had no daytime friends. We were all alone.

We got home and still Twittlebug could not nurse. She cried and cried from hunger, but could not nurse. Again, I was committed to no bottles. I had no idea why it was so important, but it was do-or-die for me. I finally called La Leche League and this angel came to our apartment. She gave me a little disk thing to wear on my breast inside my bra. It passively expressed milk, which I gave to Twittlebug via an eyedropper. She only had a little bit, but went back to sleep. The next morning my breasts were not as engorged and Twittlebug was able to latch. That was the problem that a brand new mom could not have known – my breasts were too full for my little baby to latch onto.

I will never forget that wonderful woman who left her own young family at nine at night, and came to my house and saved me. As I write this, I am welling up with tears of gratitude. I went to La Leche meetings for years and years. Not only for breastfeeding advice, but to share with other moms who had the same mothering visions as me. I remain so grateful.

Mahrigh helped me with my baby sharing her angst experience t and advice.

Moms are the best things ever, even if they're not our own. I cannot express how grateful I am for this story. It was so cathartic for me. It amazes me how women forget the pain of birth, but even after thirty years, viscerally remember their breastfeeding trials.

A woman from my birthing class was told that her nipples were "made for nursing," but she still experienced blistering and incredible soreness the first week, as well as painful engorgement. She sought help from a lactation consultant (LC), who helped her nursling latch by pulling gently on his lower lip to open his mouth wider. If he got it wrong, she would just take him off her nipple and try again. The LC said that he would figure out that with a wider latch he would get more milk. This appeared to be the case, because shortly thereafter, her nursling started fixing his lips himself to get that wide, fish-mouth latch.

Five months after My Little Milkaholic was born, in the throes of desperate loneliness and baby blues, I met Saint Monica (after the patron saint of mothers[5]) through a mommy group she'd started. She said, when her Peanut was born, they put him on her left breast and he sucked fiercely, but without a proper latch. She too was amazed at the new life she'd created, and didn't notice the damage he was doing. Luckily, she quickly got some help. "In the hospital right away, they brought me a pump so I could gather my drops of colostrum, put it in tiny syringes and feed it to Peanut. My husband would put it in the side of his mouth as Peanut was sucking at my breast. My husband's other job was to help Peanut latch properly by pulling down his little jaw. It was so difficult to get little Peanut into position, but once we were set, everything seemed to be functioning."

A saintly former professor of mine had her three nurslings at a freestanding birth center. After each birth, when she was comfortable in bed, the midwives helped her nurse. Some women who birth at a freestanding birth center go home four to six hours after having the baby - if they have successfully nursed the baby. "The approach is very empowering and encouraging," she said. New mommas get newborn care, lactation, and family support

---

5   The patron saint of breastfeeding women is a man who survived exile by drinking milk, which while cool, doesn't seem to fit here.

visits on day two, week one, and week six. The Professor's last baby gained a pound in her first week of life. She said, "They not only have a really successful birthing model at Mountain Midwifery Center and other birth centers, but a really high rate of successful breastfeeding." I have to admit hearing stories like hers makes me a bit jealous, but as the birthing centers in Colorado are not allowed to do vaginal breech births; I couldn't have had My Little Milkaholic there, anyway.

New Zealand seems to do post-natal support right, too. A saint there said:

> First of all, in New Zealand, when you are pregnant you can either decide to pay for an obstetrician (about $4,000 to $6,000 for all pre-, birth, and post-natal care), or you can get a midwife, which is one hundred percent paid for by the government. I think I was a bit naïve and thought it would all be good, so I just got a midwife. She was awesome though, a lovely woman from Yorkshire, and very medically trained. Once you have a midwife you are in the 'system' and they send you information about antenatal classes, which are in all areas of the country and free.

The same surgeon, who delivered his father by C-section in 1980, delivered Doozle Bug by

C-section; New Zealand is small. They put him right on my boob, and he was happy enough. We took him back to the ward, but his blood sugar was low, so they put him NICU overnight. To be honest, this was fine by me, as I was able to focus on recovery.

For the next couple of days I focused on starting breastfeeding. Even though they gave Doozle Bug bits of formula without question (they will do this without fuss if a baby is in NICU), they wanted me to breastfeed when I could, and gave me a lactation consultant to help me.

I established breastfeeding a week after Doozle Bug was born, while we were still in the hospital. There is no way I would have been able to do this without a lactation consultant to watch, correct and give me tips, and the full support of being in the hospital. How they expect first-time mothers, whom they boot out of the hospital within hours of giving birth, and whom they give no further support to breastfeed, is very far beyond me!

Once we got home, my midwife came to visit us two

times per week for the first six weeks. I asked her a lot of questions and raised any issues I had. She also observed me feeding and gave me more tips and tricks. Once Doozle Bug was six weeks old, we were referred to a service here called Plunket. Infant-trained nurses visit you every couple of months to weigh your baby and check in to see how feeding is going and how you are doing. They also give you a lot of advice about how and when to introduce solids.

I am very lucky to live in New Zealand, and I know that breastfeeding would not have been as easy or maybe even possible if I had had Doozle Bug in the US, the UK, or even Australia (where support is not as good as in NZ). It is interesting how different and similar it is everywhere in the world. If I had a choice, I would have my next baby in Holland. There, you are given a live-in nurse for the first week you are home – and they do cleaning as well.

It is nice to hear about women who didn't have a super hard time establishing nursing, but it seems the moral of these stories is: Have your baby somewhere where they will send women over to your house to check on you, or Holland.

In the course of joining new mom groups, I often heard

24

that the women who had taken breastfeeding classes while they were pregnant were more prepared than I. The classes did not necessarily exempt them from problems, but primed the women to get help right away. Makes sense.

For me, breastfeeding started out, what I thought was, "normally." We had a little trouble, but it seemed like we just needed some practice. I knew the first week could be hard, so I wasn't worried right away. My Little Milkaholic tried really hard, but kept popping off my nipple. I couldn't understand why he was doing it, and assumed it was just part of the process. But it only got worse.

CHAPTER 4

Screaming at the Breast

Despite being sent home by our pediatrician on day four, this time with a newly fattened, healthy baby and assurances that we could manage; I once again began to experience the fear/sadness/pain of thinking I was starving my baby.

Breastfeeding was not going well.

My Little Milkaholic screamed when I tried to give him my boob. Wasn't he hungry?

And he screamed. Why didn't he just stay on?!

And he screamed. How could God give me this being if I couldn't keep him alive?

The Best Husband Ever and our extended family held (and fed) him, while I pumped and rested and cried. They were all very supportive. My mother-in-law tried to reassure me with stories of baby Best Husband Ever's difficulty latching. But, I was exhausted, overwhelmed and unprepared, so it wasn't cathartic.

At times, my fear and anxiety were all consuming. I was so tired, and all I could think was that it shouldn't be *this* hard. But it was. Frankly, I'm not sure how anyone can be prepared for breastfeeding in general and latch difficulties in particular.

At first, I would try to nurse My Little Milkaholic for twenty to thirty minutes at a time. After about a week or so of him screaming every time I tried to feed him, and so easily taking the bottle, I quit trying so hard. After about five to ten minutes – depending on how quickly he turned to screaming – I would pass him off to be bottle-fed, so that I could pump. It was an efficient routine, but not one that allowed me to bond with my baby.

I so badly wanted to breastfeed, but I would get enormously frustrated and worried about what I might do. I wasn't worried about shaken baby syndrome. I was worried about thrown baby syndrome. No matter how rational you are (and in that first month, with hormones controlling you like a puppet, you are not particularly rational), it is hard not to take it personally when your baby screams every time you try to nurse him.

If you haven't been through it, imagine holding your nursling with one hand, squeezing your breast with the other and shoving it in your nursling's mouth. But then he pops off and cries because he is hungry. Something isn't working, but he can't tell you what. So you keep at it for as long as you can take it, taking every second of quiet suckling as a blessing, but praying for fifteen consecutive minutes of feeding, because that is how long a doctor or nurse said you were supposed nurse. Once you finally give up, you either hand the baby over to a daddy or friend or family member, so they can peacefully feed the baby you're supposed to be able to serenely suckle. Or, you give up any break time you would have had and bottle-feed your nursling so you get some amount of bonding time, and then you hook your semi-raw nipples to suction cups.

The pump stimulates your breasts, and sucks out as much milk as it can, which often is not as much as you'd like, and not nearly what a baby would get by suckling. You pump for ten to fifteen minutes. Sterilize the equipment. Put everything away. Take a break long enough to slather your nipples with lanolin, and hopefully, eat something and get a little more tranquil bonding while your baby sleeps before the whole process starts over again. Repeat every two or three hours, day and night, for two or three months.

Saint Monica from the mommy group said it well: "It is a very real awakening to realize how much time it takes to nurse, and then pump to encourage more production. It is literally constant, around the clock, every day for weeks and weeks." It is a process that makes using formula a perfectly rational choice, but then so many of us endure even for a few days, and so we deserve sainthood.

Despite our nursing ineptitude, My Little Milkaholic was growing like a world-record giant pumpkin, but the nursing was not going well. I could tell he wanted to, but we just couldn't get it to work. At his regularly scheduled appointments, our pediatric PA-LC continued to try to assist me in nursing. She suggested that my nipples were too flat and gave me a nipple shield – a thin silicone (clear plastic-like) nipple-shaped cover, that fits over the nipple, extending it slightly to the back of the baby's mouth to facilitate feeding[6]. It's like training wheels for the breastfeeding uncoordinated, and sometimes it worked. But mostly we ended up giving up after he would pull it off and scream.

Breastfeeding was definitely not the blissful bonding time I'd expected. When the nipple shield worked, it was a feat of coordination: juggling the baby, while holding my breast and putting the nipple shield on (and on again when he pulled it off), and keeping myself covered when we had visitors. I think I'm now coordinated enough to juggle, chew gum and ride a bike, all at the same time. (I've often been accused of not being able to walk and chew gum.)

Nights were the worst. Fighting with a screaming, starving baby in the middle of the night is enough to drive the sanest person to a breakdown. It felt as if the Best Husband Ever got to cuddle *my* baby, while I nursed a machine. Or if I decided to try to feed him, I was up for more than an hour at every feeding, attempting to nurse and then pumping. So we generally skipped the breast at night. We worked out a two-shift night system, so we both could get some sleep. The Best Husband Ever slept in our bedroom from 9 p.m. until 3 or 4 a.m., while I was on duty, napping between feedings on the futon in the baby cave (our version of a nursery/library/office/my closet). Then he took over in the baby cave until 9 a.m., and I slept in our bedroom. We both got about six hours of

---

6   Nipple shields are great for super-fast let-down and engorgement. The nipple part holds a bit of milk allowing the baby to control how fast they it, and it helps them get the right mouth position when your boobs are too swollen and hard to get a proper latch.

sleep a night and felt nearly functional.

Having heard stories about babies not latching from a cousin and a couple friends, I thought I was being smart and open minded in understanding that not everyone can breastfeed. And, by My Little Milkaholic's one-month birthday, I was thinking about giving up. I figured as long as he was getting my milk, the delivery method didn't really matter.

The most interesting phenomenon of motherhood to me is the complete lack of time perspective. At a month old, My Little Milkaholic seemed so grown up to me. I had expected that he would sleep through the night and smile and babble; things apparently six-month-olds do. Looking back, I laugh at how little and unformed he was. But at the time, a month seemed like the longest span. I couldn't imagine why people kept saying childhood goes by so fast. The first month went by so slowly. He must be old and have the hang of this living thing, I thought, and if he wasn't breastfeeding by then, he wasn't going to. Silly me.

It was during the 3 a.m. feedings that my plan to be an exclusive pumper fell apart. My Little Milkaholic outpaced what I could pump, so I had to pump at every feeding. I had tear-filled visions of pumping every three hours for the rest of my life and of never-ending engorgement pain[7]. I wasn't strong enough to exclusively pump; I couldn't imagine how other women did it. I fought off resentment. Luckily, desperation is a great motivator.

---

7   I didn't yet know that my body would adjust and my milk supply would decrease to a reasonable amount.

The next day, and the New Year, my quest began; I would breastfeed My Little Milkaholic if it killed me. While shopping for diaper wraps, I perused breastfeeding chapters in books for new mommies, only to find advice on what to do if your baby falls asleep feeding (wake them up). They skipped the part about how to get your baby to latch in the first place! But all the books did recommend setting aside long periods of time for feedings so that neither of us felt rushed. Then I spoke to the store sales clerk, who said that her two year-old had been a breast screamer, but she hadn't ever given him a bottle. She couldn't remember how she got him to latch, but at least I learned it was possible. I mean, he *was* still alive and running around the store like a maniac after all.

At home, I turned to Dr. Google. Searching for "baby screaming at the breast," I only found two blog posts that addressed my specific issue. They said to create a calm place for feedings, and counter to everything I'd been told to that point, not force it. Even as a toddler, My Little Milkaholic spits out anything we shove in his mouth, so it makes sense that I had to let him come to it on his own. One blogger, The Lactivist, said to let him suckle on my finger (she was anti-pacifier) to calm him down first, then try the breast gently. Eager to try this new advice, I sat at the computer and tried to feed him. He didn't latch, but letting him suckle my finger and a pacifier (I am not anti-pacifier), kept us both calm and gave me hope for future feedings.

And, then I starved him for six hours.

It was not intentional, of course. I had decided not to give him the bottle option at all. We were going cold turkey. If the clerk at the baby store could do it, so could we! It had been about three hours since his last feeding, when I tried the bloggers' suggestions. And we had a doctor's appointment shortly thereafter, so I couldn't spend hours working with him. The Best Husband Ever, sensing my, let's say fervor (I was a woman possessed), took the position of yes-man, and let me make the decisions about feeding My Little Milkaholic that day. It takes a strong, smart man to know when he can't fix something and just let it go.

My Little Milkaholic wasn't fussy at all that afternoon, despite the skipped meals and manhandling by the orthopedist[8]. We had been overfeeding him for a month; turns out he will (still does) drink as much milk as we are able/willing to give him. So, he probably could have skipped eating for a day or two and been just fine.

When we got home that late afternoon, My Little Milkaholic and I sat down to feed. I prepared with a magazine and water for me, and nipple shield and pacifier for him. I settled in for endurance breastfeeding training. And it worked! We started with a pacifier, and then I gently gave him my silicone-covered nipple, and he latched and ate like we'd been starving him for hours, which we kind of had been. He fed like the breast was all he ever wanted; like it was the most natural thing ever; and he fed for nearly an hour. I was in heaven! The physical relief of

---

8   Pediatricians recommend breech babies have their hips examined by ultra sound to ensure they don't have hip dysplasia. My Little Milkaholic was perfectly formed.

having fully drained boobs cannot be overstated, and of course I'd accomplished my goal and was bonding with my baby like I'd imagined I was supposed to.

We stuck to it, and he almost became good at nursing. Despite a month of nearly exclusive bottle-feeding, and a week with a nipple shield, My Little Milkaholic had no nipple confusion[9]; he would take milk wherever he could get it. We moved him back into our room and nursed every feeding. I do not have the words to describe my relief. I had made it. I was breastfeeding. I relaxed for the first time in a month; I could finally keep my baby alive.

---

9   The Guru, the Lactation Consultant/Proprietress of a Denver momma support center, said that all babies want to nurse, and with enough time and effort they can. Some have nipple (bottle) preferences, but those can be overcome. (Now, whether or not you have the where-with-all to work through nursing problems with a stubborn baby is another story.)

CHAPTER 5

The Good, the Bad and the Ugly of Pumping

I cannot express how much I hated pumping. Just before My Little Milkaholic latched, I was convinced I would have to pump every three hours for the rest of my life, my personal version of Sisyphus and his rock. Physically, it made me nauseous, logistically it was a pain, and emotionally it made me feel like a dairy cow. It was so bad that I considered giving up cheese in solidarity with my dairy cow sisters. But I didn't, because I love cheese and am human and can just choose not to pump. Sorry, cows, I suck. A friend of mine from grad school decided to eat meat-lite and cruelty free, and is avoiding milk because he said, "industrial milk cows are practically tortured." I feel their pain.

Apparently, I'm not alone in feeling like a dairy cow. Saint Adele, the wife of a coworker of The Best Husband Ever, said that at one point while she was pumping and looking at herself in the bathroom mirror at work, she thought she must be going crazy because she felt like her breast pump was becoming her best friend. When she had her second child, her first child was able to imitate the sound of the breast pump. "Most kids imitate car or truck sounds or animal sounds, but not Biscuit," she said. "She would walk around the house and make the sound the pump would make as I pumped, and when I'd ask her what she was playing, she would say 'the cow sound, mommy.'" Perhaps cows are sacred in India because the mommas there relate.

Saint Elizabeth, a friend in Utah, had a really hard time figuring out how to use her pump. "I had a bad attitude about the whole pumping thing to begin with," she said. "It is difficult to not feel like a cow. When I finally got it to work, I freaked out. I thought the milk would come out in a single stream. I had no idea that you had multiple ducts, and I thought there was something wrong with me that I had multiple streams of milk. My husband found the whole thing to be immensely funny."

The breast pump, like birth control, is simultaneously the best and worst invention ever. It allows women to have jobs and careers away from their babies, stimulate milk production, and effectively gives us more control over our lives and how we feed our babies, but it is also a gigantic pain in the ass. If you have not had the pleasure of researching pumps, there are basically three kinds: hospital-grade electric, regular electric pumps and hand pumps. Hospital-grade pumps have the most power, but are about the size and weight of a Coach tote filled with rocks, and have all the style of a plastic grocery bag. Electric pumps vary in power from brand to brand, but operate mostly the same and come in one or two breast-pumping styles. Two breast attachments are faster as you can do both sides at once, but can be a bit intense. Some come with bra attachments for hands-free pumping, which makes sense because, seriously, have you tried to not use your hands for ten to fifteen minutes? Hand pumping seems a million times harder, like manual labor, but I never tried it – hand pumping that is. I've done manual labor. The Best Husband Ever said, "They are just like man tools – contractor grade, electric and old school hand tools. The contractor is too powerful and nobody has the time to actually use a hand tool!!"

My saintly Friend with Twins had her babies three weeks early, and so they spent a while in the NICU. "The wonderful nurses there immediately helped me start pumping with an electric pump so they could freeze my milk," she said. When not at the hospital, they used a hand pump because they didn't have access to an electric one. I say "they" because her husband did the pumping for her! She was so engorged and exhausted, and "He thought that it was pretty fascinating," she said. Seems only fair.

An amazing author friend told me she once forgot to bring her pump to a conference she'd traveled to. She said, "I had to manually milk myself like a cow, because my boobs were enormous and dripping." So, she tugged and sprayed milk into a towel in her hotel room. We do what we have to.

For the first month of My Little Milkaholic's life, I used a rented hospital-grade pump, and then bought a Modela Freelance Pump because it's über portable and because I work as a freelance writer. At the time, it seemed perfect. So many half thoughts and delusions. The first was that I would be able and willing to start working again right after I gave birth. It took me until My

Little Milkaholic was five months old before I had the energy and brainpower to write again, not to mention any willingness to leave him with a nanny[10].

When I bought the pump, I had a vague image of pumping while I worked. But when the fog of hormones lifted and I regained my ability think full thoughts, I realized I couldn't work with the baby around. Pumping while sitting in a coffee shop, sipping a decaf latte and typing just seemed super awkward. Instead, I pumped and watched *Buffy the Vampire Slayer* for the first month until My Little Milkaholic latched, and then I tried not to pump as much as possible.[11]

Of course, choosing not to pump is not an option many women are willing to take; pumps are portable and designed to prolong breastfeeding after all. A saintly preschool teacher told me she used to pump in a storage closet at work that had a temperature variance of forty to ninety degrees. She put a sign on the door and wore a coat in the winter. But it allowed her to work full time and still feel connected to her nursling.

Another friend a year ahead of us, Saint Saeran, was unable to get her nursling to latch, so she became an exclusive pumper. For two months at work, she set up a little pumping station in

---

10   I had a decent bout of baby blues, which impacted my getting back to work, but ultimately it took a good friend watching him to get me back on my feet. - Her saint of a momma saw my need and encouraged her to help me. I'm telling you, those mommas, our own and our friends' are just amazing!

11   Not wanting to pump made it less relevant that my regular pump pulled less milk than the hard-core hospital rental pump.

the bathroom, partitioned with a curtain and furnished with a comfy chair, a desk and a refrigerator. She blocked her calendar three times a day for thirty minutes each to pump. Her boss was basically respectful about not scheduling things during those times, but didn't think twice about invading that personal time and Saeran's space. "My boss would sometimes follow me into the bathroom and talk outside of the 'curtain.' One time she joked, 'I should just come in, you have your Hooter Hider on, right?!' I probably would have pumped a little longer if my boss was more supportive of flex hours or another arrangement to allow me to pump," she said.

One of our saintly neighbors also pumped at work in the bathroom, in a "weird little alcove area" with a curtain, a club chair, a tiny table and dorm fridge. "I could hear everyone's bathroom activities – flushing, sinks, etc. – and everyone could hear the pumping machine," she said. Her office did have a small non-bathroom space available, but it didn't have a fridge. She felt weird carrying her milk through the office, and storing it the in the shared fridge with everyone's lunch, so she used the one in the restroom alcove.

One day, while sitting in the alcove minding her own business, pumping, a woman peeked in on her. "It must have shocked her – nursing bra on with pump running on both sides and me on my blackberry texting! She mumbled something about not knowing what the noise was, and I made some smart-ass comment. I hope she was as mortified as I was! I don't think I ever saw the woman again!" If women pumped in public, there would never be another negative word about women breastfeeding in public.

Though it seems rare, an RN friend from college found community in pumping at work. She said there usually were several nursing mommas in the emergency department, so they would all "cram into the one open patient room and have a pumping party. Shirts off, boobs out, pump bottles balanced on knees while we scarfed down food and drink."

Maybe we need to start a hands-free-pumping-bra drive for nurses, or well anyone who pumps. Next time you get invited to a baby shower...

The woman I bought my pump from told me she had a nurse friend who used the same kind of hands-free pump I was buying, and used to pump while she was driving to work. I imagined her driving around bare-chested, freaking out male drivers and getting thumbs up from other women. But Riona said she pumped while driving once, and no one seemed to notice. That was a level of dedication I never reached.

For all our stories about the pains of pumping and the ridiculous things we put up with to pump, it is still a great innovation. The pump allowed my cousin, Saint Jane, to feed her baby breast milk, even though she wasn't able to nurse him, though it wasn't easy:

Pumping is how I got my milk to come in, since Baby Man wasn't getting the job done. We had to give him some formula the first few days. Our lactation consultant and midwives were worried he'd get dehydrated and what a shame to have to go to the hospital because of that, after having a wonderful home birth experience! So, after about 30 hours of unsuccessful attempts with midwives and lactation consultants working with us on breastfeeding, I started pumping. It hurt really badly. After a few tries thinking there was no way I could do it, I read online to use olive oil for lubrication and that was a godsend. I used a Q-tip to swab olive oil on the inside of the part that goes around your boobs. That made it bearable.

I had no clue what I was doing, though. Since pumping was such a drag and I'm very type-A, I was like, oh I'll just pump both boobs at the same time, and then I won't have to do it as much. Um, no. I ended up making enough milk for twins! We had bottles and bottles in the fridge. I was stocking up in the freezer, and the milk just kept coming.

We rarely left the house during my three-and-a-half-month maternity leave. I didn't want to go anywhere because it was such a hassle to lug all the pumping gear around and to pump away from home. Plus, I was SO uncomfortable. My boobs were never the same size, and wearing a bra hurt like mad because my nipples were so sore. I would slather my nipples with that Lansinoh stuff after each pumping session and it ruined all my shirts. I really felt like a total wreck. It kind of makes me want to vomit just thinking about it! LOL!

I went back to work at three-and-a-half months. Due to the recession, things were really slow, so my boss said I could work when I had stuff to do, but otherwise I could go home if I wanted. So the first month being back at work wasn't too bad. I'd pump right before work in the morning, come home at lunch and pump, go home early and pump, pump before bed, wake up in the middle of the night to pump, wake up early in the AM to pump, then start all over again. I never even tried to pump at work. We lived literally two minutes from my office, so it was just easier to go home to do it. My colleagues were all wonderful, so it's not that it would have been weird or awkward, it was just easier to go home.

I didn't know anyone personally who only pumped like I was, so I went online and found an "Exclusive Pumpers" group. It was just a relief to know I wasn't the only person in the world doing this. I posted a couple of questions, but I wasn't really active on the group. It was just comforting to know there were lots of other women going through the same thing.

Everyone [around me] kept telling me to either give it up and feed him formula or to try nursing again. I wanted to punch anyone who told me to try nursing again. It was such an insult. I knew it was harder to pump, but it didn't make sense to try nursing again because I knew I'd have to go back to work, so I'd have to pump at that point anyway. Plus, I honestly couldn't bear the thought of trying to nurse again. It was so difficult and frustrating. I had really ugly feelings about my baby when I tried nursing. It didn't seem like a good idea to go there again. I was not in a good place physically and I think that would have pushed me over the edge. I felt pumping exclusively was the only option that would work. I really wanted Baby Man to be fed breast milk.

At four-and-a-half months, I really had to be back at work full-time. I started to slow down the pumping. We started working in formula at this point to supplement. I'd still come home at lunch and pump. I think I was pumping like only four times a day. This lasted until he was six months old. I wasn't pumping enough to keep up my supply, so at this point it kind of dried up. By then he was eating cereal and trying other baby foods, so it all kind of worked out.

Imagine the stress she would have had without the invention of the breast pump, not being able to nurse but so desperately wanting to feed her baby breast milk.

Of course, the pump doesn't work for everybody. For my saintly friend with nipples made for nursing, the pump caused more stress than it helped. She tried pumping the first week and couldn't get even an ounce from both breasts combined. "The pump was just not my friend!" she said. But, they went to a lactation consultant who measured her nursling before and after his feeding, and found that he got three to four ounces after nursing for ten to fifteen minutes[12]. Plus he'd gained weight beautifully.

Saint Adele, in New Mexico, had empty pumping

---

[12]   Research indicates exclusively breastfed babies eat an average of twenty-five ounces per day. With six to eight feedings a day, a baby will take in three to four ounces per feeding, roughly.

experiences galore before her milk came in. She pumped initially in hopes of getting more milk production so that Biscuit might want to latch better, and before each feeding to get the milk flowing, so that Biscuit didn't have to work hard to get the milk. But, it didn't really help. She would pump and literally count the drops as they came out. Like so many women I've talked to, she said, "I was thankful for the pump, but at the same time it was the bane of my new-mommy existence."

For some of us, pumping helped our production. Saint Monica said pumping early-on amplified her production, and because of it, she ended up with abundant milk. My RN friend said she pumped so much milk in the first four to five months that they had to buy an extra deep freezer for their garage. She filled something like seven grocery bags full of breast milk bags. (A workout buddy used her extra milk to supplement her husband's nutrition – she slipped it into his cereal when he wasn't looking.)

Another fellow writer's saintly wife was a pumping fiend in the first week of her baby's life. She couldn't nurse due to nipple damage, but all the pumped milk kept her baby from having to go under a bili light to raise her bilirubin.

> We had a rental bili light at the house. The challenge with the light was that the design was so horrible that I couldn't stomach leaving her in it. The thing was designed like a suitcase/briefcase, with a hinge along the backside for the case to open up. The light

itself was in the top part of the case. The way bili lights work, you need to have as much of their skin exposed as possible to the light, which meant leaving her in the thing in only her diaper. The light itself didn't put off any heat, and we couldn't bundle her to keep her warm – in Colorado in January. Add to it, there was a 'face shield' to protect her eyes from the light. In that, read, flimsy piece of fabric that hung down from the top, and was so easy for her to tear down, it was covering her face in about 5 minutes. That suffocation hazard, combined with the fact that she was so cold when on the bed, meant that she would tolerate about 5 minutes (at the most) before the really awful 'I'm incredibly upset' tears would begin.

Thank goodness for her pump!

In the first month, I pumped what felt like gallons of milk (though not enough to fill a whole deep-freezer). It almost became (a somewhat unhealthy) competition with myself to see if I could pump a personal best. I topped out at thirteen ounces in one ten-to-fifteen minute session. Though having a freezer full of milk is a very satisfying feeling, pumping does nothing for decreasing engorgement.

All the stories about pumping that I've heard just prove

how remarkable moms are. The amazing amount of awkwardness, discomfort and hassle we put up with to take care of our children is heroic. It makes one little holiday seem insufficient. (Although Mother's Day is my new favorite holiday, because I get to relax and do what I want, with no social expectations, and I get presents!) I hated pumping because of the nausea and pain and weird emotional ickiness, but it does allow mommas who cannot breastfeed to feed their babies breast milk, helps prevent and heal mastitis, and comforts our fears of not being able to feed our babies. It is a double-edged sword of terrible awesomeness.

CHAPTER 6

What the Hell Is Wrong With Your Tongue?

So, back to my breastfeeding Odyssey.

My relief at getting My Little Milkaholic to latch was palpable. I couldn't wait to feed him. I let The Best Husband Ever sleep, and took over the whole nighttime feeding routine. For like two nights. Then we moved My Little Milkaholic back to our room and The Best Husband Ever changed diapers, and then I did the feedings.

The first week of for-reals breast feeding, we used a nipple shield, and then one day we just didn't. I got lazy, and My Little Milkaholic didn't care that it wasn't there. I had been told that the first week-to-month of breastfeeding could be painful, so I prepared myself. I steeled myself against the pain, tried to relax and worked my way further through *Buffy*.

Our saintly neighbor said her (awesome) mom gave her a glass of wine for the particularly uncomfortable feedings and stocked up on gossip magazines. She said the first few weeks were agonizing for her until she found Motherlove Nipple Cream at Whole Foods that "was seriously life changing." It took a month, and the help of an LC, for latching and nursing to fall into place for her.

By the end of week two of nursing, my nipples felt like they were being held in vice grips while being licked by a cat with a sandpaper tongue over and over. I was pretty sure I could hear the scraping, but I may have been hallucinating from the pain. Both nipples were cracked and white, when they weren't bleeding. One of my best friends and saint, whose baby is now a teenager, remembered the cracks and bleeding, but didn't remember doing anything for it; it just sort of resolved itself, she'd said. My own saintly mother had nothing to offer either. She found breastfeeding me relaxing. So, hoping it would resolve itself, I grinned and bore the pain, and had fantasies of giving The Best Husband Ever the worst titty twisters of his life just so I wouldn't be alone in the pain. At my post-partum checkup, the nurse practitioner winced and worried for me; though, aside from lanolin, she didn't have any remedies either.

Someone (I think our pediatrician), told me that the gift shop at a local hospital near my house sold lanolin. When I ran out, we stopped there only to find its hours were as fleeting as Doctor Who's Tardis. I was kind of a mess. I'd had foot surgery right after my post-partum check-up, my nipples hurt, and obviously I was sleep-deprived. After having limped almost a block through the damn hospital, nearly in tears, and still obviously recovering from birth (read: fat), the maternity nurses took pity on me and gave me three sample size bottles of lanolin. There are so many things I am grateful for in life, and those nurses made the list right then and there.

Saint Monica (from the mommy group) also had similarly painful breastfeeding. About a week into nursing, her left boob became very sore, more than just the "normal" rawness and tenderness. She had a small open wound from a piece of skin that had come off the tip of her nipple the first time Peanut breastfed. It couldn't heal because he continued to suck the scab off, if it ever even got one.

I could not put any clothing on over my breasts because it hurt so bad to have anything touch my nipples. I was permanently living in a plush fleece bathrobe with my breasts out to the air. Only when someone came over would I cover up, and hope they wouldn't hug me too hard. *it hurts so much when Ayaan hugs me.*

The hospital had given me little gel pads, but when they dried they'd stick to my skin, and hurt so badly to take off. So I stopped using them pretty quickly. I didn't want to use nipple shields while nursing because I was too stubborn, and did not want to give the baby something other than my real nipple. *these are great! so cooling during those first few days when nipples are incredibly sore and painful.*

Looking back on it, I would try nipple shields. Why not? I had heard/read that you don't want to give a *But ouch!!*

49

bottle until a month of solid breastfeeding so there isn't 'nipple confusion.' But at this point, I had to admit that having an injured nipple was extremely painful and was not healing; the only way it would heal was to keep Peanut off of it.

It took about a week of offering him only my right breast and pumping the left for the wound to heal. I was happy to share some feeding duties with my husband, as he fed him my milk in a bottle for that week. Then an angel tipped me off that there are things better than what the hospital gave me to relieve my nipples. All I wanted was to be able to put something over my breasts when Peanut wasn't on them! Exactly three weeks after Peanut was born, I put the order in for Avent Breast Shell[13]. These things saved my life and put me back in clothes. And they caught my milk when I was leaking.

I, too, had used the gel pads to protect my nipples in an attempt to treat the pain. I kept them in the fridge (as I swear the directions said to do), and alternated throughout the day. The cold was kind of invigorating, and kind of

yup, they're great! the LC in the hospital gave me Medela brand shells

---

13   Comfort breast shells are like clam shells for your boobs, with holes for your nipples and a hard case to protect them.

Medela's nipple cream[50] worked amazingly well too.

numbing. But taking them off recreated any pain that might have been relieved.

My nipples hurt longer and longer after feedings, to the point that they never stopped hurting. At night my nipple pain began to radiate around my back along my bra-line and lasted for hours, so that I could not get back to sleep after feeding My Little Milkaholic. Once again, I fell apart at the 3 a.m. feeding. When I flashed a thought of throwing My Little Milkaholic across the room to get him off my nipples, I decided that that much pain wasn't normal. Breastfeeding would not be trendy or "natural" if everyone had this kind of pain.

While scarfing down cheese crackers – my favorite middle-of-the-night snack[14] – I again turned to Dr. Google. What did women do at 3 a.m. before the Internet? The mommy blogs relieved my hypochondria with tales of painfully cracked and bloody nipples (that should be a band name), due to vasospasm and shallow latch (also good band names). They told of remedies of warm, dry heat (not cold!) and Advil. As the actual cause and treatment were harder to ascertain, I determined to find help in the morning. In the meantime, I heated a sinus mask and laid it on my chest. Ah! The relief was like the heavenly sound of angels singing! Even my back pain subsided. *I used a heating pad which was great!*

Thanks to The Affordable Healthcare Act, health insurance companies are now required to cover LC services and breast

me too!!

---

14   For the first couple months I was so hungry after breastfeeding that I would have eaten The Best Husband Ever if he'd come between me and food. Luckily, he is well trained and ensured there were quick easy snacks available.

pumps. This means more women are getting the help we need, but it also means lactation consultants are busy. The third LC I called (referred by Google, but approved of by everyone I'd talked to), said she was sure she knew what my problem was, and rushed me in within an hour of my call. You gotta love a person who gets excited to alleviate your pain.

The LC (hereafter known as The Guru, as everyone I met in Denver swears by her advice and jokingly claims membership in her cult) was like a warm, motherly angel. She's the kind of woman that you wish was your mom, even if you have an awesome mom. I wanted to tell her everything, and cry, and have her hug me and make it all better. She ushered me into her cozy office with its big soft couch, piles of Boppies, a changing table, scale, a tiny desk, and bookshelves full of books on nursing,

I sobbed my story of the screaming unlatchable baby, ending with the bittersweet victory of the painful latch. With the enthusiasm of Mary Poppins, she looked at my mangled nipples and said she knew exactly what it was, but wanted to check other things to verify the three-pronged diagnosis before telling me. I was in so much pain and had so much hope of relief that I wasn't even terribly uncomfortable hanging out topless with this virtual stranger. I waited in rapt anticipation as she weighed My Little Milkaholic and assured me there was an easy fix. She examined his mouth, noting his upper lip callouses (which were supposed to last only a week or less, but had persisted for six-plus weeks), and had me feed him to see his/our technique. Then she told me that "normal" breastfeeding should not fall higher than a three on a zero-to-ten pain-scale. I was at a five on a good day and an eight at 3 a.m.

Her diagnosis was in: He was tongue-tied. Unlike the alarming pictures of tongues tied from tip to gums (she showed me so I wouldn't Google it when I was all alone), My Little Milkaholic had a posterior tie, which meant his little frenulum (the thing in the very back underside of your tongue that seems designed to keep you from swallowing your tongue), was too tight. This caused him to feed with his lips, which resulted in him flattening my nipple, which then cut off the blood supply causing vasospasm, which is extremely painful. It is called Raynaud's of the Nipple[15]. She assured me that getting My Little Milkaholic's tongue fixed, a two-minute procedure by a dentist, would solve our problems and that I would heal in a week or two. Then she tried to call in some favors to get him in to see the dentist that afternoon.

In anticipation of meeting The Guru, I had hoped at most for new positioning or some secret technique that I had been missing. Knowing that there was something legitimately wrong, something fixably wrong, was more than I'd imagined. I started to breathe again. I hadn't realized I'd stopped, but knowing this

---

15   Olsen and Nelsen wrote an article in the Scandinavian Journal of Clinical Lab Investigations in 1978 that said that Raynaud's of the nipple most commonly affects breastfeeding women, with onset typically occurring sometime in the first month, or during the first winter of breastfeeding and is more common in cold climates. Therefore, I think we should all be given a trip to Hawaii or someplace warm when we're breastfeeding.

wasn't just the normal pain of the first few weeks was such a relief.

Since it was Friday, The Guru was unable to get us an appointment with the dentist until the following Monday, so she let me cry out my relief, and then sent me home with a directive to bottle-feed until my nipples healed. She also gave me a list of remedies to help heal my nipples, including a regimen of magnesium, calcium, and B6; a Hydrocortisone/Polysporin topical mixture; coconut oil to lubricate the pump; and hand warmers to wear between my pad and bra. Heaven is the feeling of hand warmers on sore nipples.

If nursing were easy, there wouldn't be so many helpful products. Though breastfeeding is supposed to be the most natural thing ever, it seems like a rich-people sport for all the stuff we buy to help: nipple shields, breast pump, forty sets of pump accessories to get the right-sized pump attachments, booby cover, lanolin, gel pads, bra pads, nursing bras and tops. The Colorado Coalition for the Homeless takes opened packages of many items, so I was able to donate extra disposable diapers, pump accessories, and unused gel pads and bra pads, which made me feel a little less wasteful. Also, the thought of homeless women going through this makes me cry, so I give as much stuff as I can.

Though I have taken vitamins off and on my whole life, taking the calcium and B6 was the first time I had ever noticed an immediate reaction. Instantaneously, the pain from vasospasm decreased. The magnesium helped too, but mostly made me nauseous, so I didn't take it for very long.

We got My Little Milkaholic's tongue fixed that following Monday, despite The Best Husband Ever's mild apprehension about having it done. He was developing a growing distrust of doctors as a result of having to battle them throughout my pregnancy, and was not convinced until I was finally able to feed My Little Milkaholic pain-free. But, being the smart man he is, he continued to let me take the lead on everything breastfeeding.

The dentist sets aside an hour a day just for frenectomies[16] making them seem common. The actual occurrence of tongue-tie is unknown because it often is not diagnosed, but is estimated to be around ten percent of the population. However, when you hang out in lactation groups where people seek help, they seem way more common.

Saint Adele, in New Mexico, had had problems with tongue-tie as well:

I had read quite a bit of information about nursing and the like, but quite frankly, when nursing did NOT go well, and I tried to find written information about ways to help myself, there was not much to be found.

Our birth experiences have been long and hard, and I never would have imagined that having a baby that won't nurse well is actually MUCH harder than long,

---

16   I had hoped the word was frenulumectomy cause it's more fun to say. The professional word is ankyloglossia, which I also like.

hard labor. Our doula/CNM (certified nurse-midwife) recommended that we start nursing immediately after giving birth to try and get things moving in the right direction.

The doula was great and helped teach me how to hold Biscuit (different positions), and she helped manipulate my breast and Biscuit's mouth for about an hour right after giving birth. During this time, Biscuit did not latch well, if at all. The doula left shortly after this first breastfeeding lesson to attend to another birth. Thankfully, before she left, she spoke with one of the nurses and mentioned that I probably needed more help with nursing because things had not gone well with the first attempt.

Over the course of the next thirty-six hours, I attempted to nurse at least every hour, and these "attempts" lasted for about thirty minutes each. I was absolutely exhausted after the first several attempts – mentally, physically and emotionally. I was starting to panic a bit about the fact that our Biscuit was screaming for food, and I was seemingly NOT able to meet this need.

We did not give any bottles to her at the hospital, and I stayed the course with attempting to get her to latch. Biscuit did not latch. Period. I tried six to eight different holding positions. I tried pumping beforehand so that the milk was ready to just flow out. I tried massaging Biscuit's bottom lip with my nipple to get her mouth to "open up." Nothing seemed to work.

One thing to be thankful for is that New Mexico is HUGELY supportive of breastfeeding. At the hospital, midwives deliver all of the babies unless there are issues, and then an OB will deliver the baby. The hospital also has three lactation consultants on staff and one on duty all the time so that you can receive help anytime.

I became well known to the lactation consultants because I was determined to breastfeed, no matter how hard it was. In the hours following the birth, they visited about every three hours and would help me try to get Biscuit to latch for about thirty to forty-five minutes each time. It was during one of those sessions that one of them mentioned the use of a nipple shield to me. My first reaction was "no way" because I didn't want anything else to have to "work through" while nursing. One of the lactation consultants said that she recommended the nipple shield because she thought it might give Biscuit something to "feel" in her mouth to motivate her for more milk. Her thinking was to start nursing with it on, and then take it off as Biscuit started nursing better. She also told me that there may be issues with trying to "wean" Biscuit from it, and this was the main reason that I did not take to the idea right away.

My nursing issue did not have to do with me not having a big enough nipple; it was really about Biscuit not latching. As we prepared to go home, one of the lactation consultants mentioned that we might consider having Biscuit's frenulum cut to allow her tongue to curve and form around the nipple better. Once again, my initial thought was "no way." I didn't want anything else to complicate things. They were already difficult enough. By the time we were discharged from the hospital (after a day and a half), Biscuit had had only one poopy diaper and two wet diapers. Not a good way to head home.

The first week at home was an absolute nightmare! So much so, that at the end of day five after being home with our new blessing, I was in a heap on the kitchen floor – crying hysterically and at my wit's end. I was physically, emotionally and psychologically done. She would scream and actually try and push me away. She was good about trying every time even though it was torture for her.

Biscuit was still not nursing well and it was becoming very apparent that she was not receiving enough (if any) food from me, and she was always hungry because of it. Her crying fueled my anxiety and heartbreak. My husband called our doula after finding me on the floor in the kitchen, and she drove an hour (one way) to our home to try and help. She prayed for both of us, and then had me get in bed into a comfortable position, and she once again tried helping Biscuit latch. She looked me in the eyes and said, "I am not leaving until your baby is nursing." This put me at ease, and within about thirty minutes Biscuit was nursing a little bit. She still cried A LOT when I would put her to my breast, but she would at least try and latch a bit. At the end of two hours, our doula had mentioned that we might consider using the nipple shield just to motivate Biscuit to stay on the breast. By now, I was desperate to get breastfeeding going so we tried it, and she did "latch" – enough to get something from me, though nothing close to a full feeding.

Over the next several days, weeks and months, we continued a constant process of three-hour cycles. The first forty-five minutes was always trying to breastfeed, followed by nursing with the nipple shield, and then pumping. By the time this was all done, I had about thirty minutes before the cycle started again. Needless to say, this was exhausting. But we stayed the course.

The tongue issue "resolved" itself on its own, and I eventually was able to wean Biscuit off of the nipple shield at around four or five months. Her frenulum stretched and grew as she grew.

Since The Best Husband Ever and I failed epically at breastfeeding preparation, we did not have any preconceived ideas about the right and wrong way to feed My Little Milkaholic. So

I jumped on any intervention that would keep him alive and help me feed him, including the frenectomy. But I still had my own weird fixations. The Guru told me tongue-tie was congenital, so of course I wanted to know whose side of the family to blame. Apparently, back in the day, before doctors convinced our mothers and grandmothers that breastfeeding was unnatural and spread germs, everyone breastfed and knew what troubles ran in families and how to fix them. I pretended I wanted to know where the tongue-tie came from to warn both my or The Best Husband Ever's little sisters, but I think it was probably to pin the blame for my pain on someone, even though it really didn't matter. I fought so hard to be considered relevant in the whole process of having My Little Milkaholic that I wanted to hold someone responsible for this random new torture.

Talking to my mom, stepmom and mother-in-law, I discovered evidence that suggests The Best Husband Ever may have been tongue-tied, and that was why my mother-in-law had had so much trouble breastfeeding him. It also explained his dental problems as a kid, which The Guru and the dentist said could be avoided by My Little Milkaholic having the frenectomy. (Of course, it turns out the early teething comes from my side of the family, so I was probably doomed to painful nursing no matter what.)

The procedure was quite simple. The dentist put some numbing stuff on two long Q-tips and applied it to the area around My Little Milkaholic's frenulum, then snipped the frenulum with a tiny pair of scissors. My Little Milkaholic was a champ. He smiled at the dentist until the snip, and then screamed like hell until I got him on my boob, then drank like he'd never drunk before. Some women reported to The Guru that the pain went away immediately. I was pretty damaged, so I can't say that, but it definitely was better. His bleeding stopped after a bit of feeding, and we all went home an exhausted, but healing family.

CHAPTER 7

Nursing Mothers Do it in Groups

Despite The Guru's promise of continued help, I had some anxiety over attending lactation groups. I need to confess that I am not one of those people comfortable being naked, let alone in public. I don't skinny-dip; rarely walk around the house naked, and was not comfortable nursing uncovered around people.

I admire people who are comfortable naked. A saintly RN friend had a house rule: if you don't want to see boobs then get out. She refused to cover up at home and even answered the door one time with her baby on her boob and signed for a package. "The delivery guy was standing as far back as he could while handing me the pen," she said. I, on the other hand, sought privacy in our bedroom or the baby cave when it was time to nurse.

So the thought of hanging with a bunch of women with their breasts hanging out was not appealing to me, and was probably one reason it took me so long to get help when My Little Milkaholic wouldn't latch. The other reason I didn't go to Lactation groups was a weird idea that it was just a bunch of women nursing together, not a formally organized situation to get help. Despite talking to Saeran, who had gone to a lactation group to get help, I had weird misconceptions. I pictured women nursing at school desks because during my birthing class I saw the room the lactation groups met in, and it was filled with desks. I apparently didn't ask the detailed, logistical questions.

So, going to a lactation group meeting was daunting for me. The Guru's promise helped, alleviating one of my misconceptions, and yet I retained a mental image of women with happily suckling babies, and me with a screaming baby disrupting everyone. And, I was afraid of hearing all the same positioning tips that I'd heard from my PA-LC that hadn't worked. Not reading anything about screaming babies in any book, I felt as if I was the only one with my problems. Of course, intellectually, I knew that couldn't be the case, and The Guru had assured me I wasn't alone, but I had spent a month-and-a-half reinforcing my aloneness.

The day after My Little Milkaholic's frenectomy, I went to my first lactation group. I was late, frazzled, having transportation problems, and was still in pain. I was a mess. For the record, I am not one of those cute mommas that make looking like a mess look good with designer sweatpants and cute sandals and the perfect messy up-do. I'm the pit-stained, stringy haired mess, still in slippers because I forgot about shoes altogether[17]. And I probably have something in my teeth – don't even ask when I had last brushed my teeth.

I snuck in the large yoga-style room, which had soft wood

---

17   The Best Husband ever read that and said he loves me anyway! Admittedly, I may have dyed my hair florescent yellow on accident right before our first date, so I set his expectations low.

floors, bare but some shelves, and – thankfully – covered mirrors, and squeezed into the circle. The group had just begun going around the circle and introducing themselves, and asking their breastfeeding questions. In my mind, I was prepared for the skin and boobs of a topless bar. In reality, most of the women sat in the circle, and either nursed their babies quietly and discreetly or waited for help and their turn to talk fully covered. Some of the nursing women used covers or blankets, most didn't, and all put their boobs away when their nurslings finished. The most skin in the room was from the naked babies getting weighed pre- and post-feeding and a couple of diaper-only "movers" who escaped their mothers' grasps. There is more cleavage at a dance club than there was in that lactation group.

The fact is, lactation groups exist because breastfeeding is hard, and everyone there has, or has had problems. Yes, there are boobs, but generally everyone is discreet and paying more attention to wiggly babies and the stories being shared than each other's mommy parts.

When The Guru diagnosed me, she told me to take the weekend off from breastfeeding to let myself heal. Ever the overachiever (and never one to whine over a little pain), I tried to feed My Little Milkaholic then and there. And I cried. I cried because it still hurt. I cried because I was around other people and could no longer contain my emotions. I cried because I was hormonal. I cried because I was late and disheveled. (I am even tearing up as I write this, just at the memory of it all.) I was so overwhelmed. But I listened, to, while I cried. And a sweet new momma's momma seated next to me assured me that it was going to be OK.

The twenty to thirty women in the group covered the gamut of issues. There were mommas there worried about their day-old babies' weight loss and their own under-production of milk. There were a few celebrating new baby weight gains and dealing with over-production of milk. There were mommas dealing with palate issues, teething problems, and women who just needed general support and assurances. There was even a woman there for support as she induced milk production so she could breastfeed her adopted baby girl. How awesome is that?! And I was one of quite a few suffering from tongue-tie-related injuries.

When it was my turn to share, the group broke up to talk to each other and get personal help. The Guru came over and apologized for missing me. And then she convinced me to hold off on breastfeeding for the rest of the week to let myself heal, sweetly assuaging my fear that my window would close with her oft repeated quote, "Babies want to breastfeed." (I'm just saying, but if a woman can nurse her adopted baby girl, no problem is unsolvable!) Then she taught me to tease My Little Milkaholic with the bottle and pacifier, making him pull them in with his tongue to teach him how to feed with his tongue properly.

The week or so that I took off to heal was both a great relief and really hard. It was fantastic to not be in pain, but it meant nighttime feedings took longer, so The Best Husband Ever and I were both sleep-deprived again. And I was pumping again. Blech. After about a week or so of "healing," my nipples were looking more ragged than before. Despite the oily gooeyness of my healing paste, and coconut oil pump lubrication, I had dry callous-like blisters around the areola – white, crusty, dead skin on my nipple tips and bright redness everywhere else. My nipples didn't hurt though, and when I started breastfeeding again My Little Milkaholic didn't seem to mind, though when a piece of skin came off and he swallowed it his eyes would get all big like, "What the hell was that?"

It should be pointed out here that I am a hypochondriac – when I'm healthy – but when something might actually be wrong I rationalize it away. When My Little Milkaholic was six months old I got shingles. But it took me two weeks to go to the doctor because I was convinced that the pox were spider bites (my house got a thorough cleaning hunting for those damn spiders), and when they spread, I was sure it was either more bites or the spiders had laid eggs in me and the eggs had hatched and were eating me (did I say I was rational? I might have meant...something else). A friend did not buy my rationale, and when I went to the doctor at her suggestion, he confirmed that spiders in Colorado don't lay eggs in you.

The point is, after a week-and-a-half, my nipples seemed to be getting worse (not painful, but gross looking) rather than better. I thought since they call it Raynaud's of the nipple that it was like frostbite and the dead skin just needed to be shed (though that might not actually be true about frostbite either; I don't remember). So I wasn't worried when my nipples turned white and scaly, and I thought the blisters were from pumping. If you haven't had the chance to pump, let me clarify that though there is some friction as the suction pulls your nipple into the funnel like breast shields[18], it shouldn't cause blisters, especially with a lubricant.

I went back to see The Guru. And feeling big sisterly, I brought along my poor unsuspecting sister-in-law, who was visiting. I thought she should know about all I was going through in case she too had the tongue-tie gene and had these problems with her future babies. In retrospect I should have brought a camera. The Guru wanted me to take pictures of my nipples; I wish I'd gotten a picture of her face. As I peeled off the paste-filled gel pads, The Guru's jaw dropped. She tried to recover in the name of professionalism, but her eyes grew like the Grinch's heart. She stared and analyzed and marveled. I laughed.

Again I was relieved that I wasn't just being a hypochondriac; plus I have always enjoyed being the patient that stumps medical professionals and doesn't fit into those perfect little statistical boxes. It's practically a hobby for me. She had never seen nipples that f*d up before. She wasn't sure what to do with me. Worried it was thrush (a yeast infection), though confused because My Little Milkaholic showed no signs and I wasn't in pain, she began calling doctors to see if anyone could take a

---

18   The pump flanges (the things your boobs go in) come in difference sizes. I was apparently way bigger than I thought, as The Guru moved me up to the biggest flange, which cut down on the friction.

culture. Of course it was a Friday again. My OB couldn't get me in until the next week since he has a thriving practice (he is one of the only doctors in Colorado that still delivers breech babies and one in twenty-five babies are breech, so he's a busy man), so she got me in with a general practitioner near her office. She also got my pediatrician to call in a prescription for thrush for My Little Milkaholic, and fretted over my new, unidentified issue. We agreed to forgo my gel pasties, and she released me to go see the doctor she'd contacted for testing.

On the way out, I felt the need to educate my sister-In-law – despite her insistence that she did not need to be exposed – and flashed her my gross nipples, which were slightly less gross at that point. I mean if you can't show off your gross flesh-eating virus, what fun is it? She turned away with a mix or horror and discomfort. And, like (what I assume is) a proper southern lady, she repressed the memory, and to this day says it never happened. (The Best Husband also pretends – with a cringe – that he doesn't remember.)

The new doctor took a culture, which came back negative. Turns out My Little Milkaholic and I were fine, well he was, anyway. I was having an allergic reaction to the paste that was supposed to be healing me. Once I quit using it, I healed up for real and I began, once again, happily breastfeeding My Little Milkaholic – every two hours, and even comfortably in The Guru's lactation group.

CHAPTER 8

Mastitis, Engorgement and Other Pains in the Boob

When I found out I was pregnant, I decided I would not get fat. I read that there was no reason to gain more than twenty-five pounds, and since I had already gained ten pounds being married, I figured I only needed to gain fifteen pounds. (It's ok, you can laugh at me.) I tried counting calories, but realized I stopped eating when I was keeping track and that made me sick[19]. So, I quit tracking how much I ate and just focused on eating healthy and exercising.

I ran until thirty-three weeks (once My Little Milkaholic turned breech it became very painful to run), and did yoga throughout my pregnancy. By thirty-nine weeks, when My Little Milkaholic was born, I'd gained forty pounds, on top of my marriage ten. I swelled! I was huge! And there was nothing I could do about it, except believe all the liars who said the weight comes off "quickly" when you breastfeed[20].

---

19   While pregnant we're supposed to eat 300 more calories than a normal healthy diet, and while breastfeeding we're supposed to eat 500 more calories.

20   By quickly, what people really mean is that if you work hard you can lose it in the same amount of time it took you to put it on.

When my pregnancy boobs came in, I thought surely D/DD was as big as my poor little (previously B/C) boobs could grow. Oh, how wrong I was. Again. After we finally got breastfeeding down, I went to buy nursing bras (as I was popping out of the C cup hand-me-downs I had), and was measured at an E cup, which I didn't even know existed.

Pregnant, I enjoyed my new cleavage and imagined with some amount of horror how much bigger my boobs would be when my milk came in. I eased my fears with images of myself with a Barbie Doll figure by the spring (four months or so after giving birth seemed like plenty of time to get in shape to me). Given how voluptuous I was, I'm pretty sure that if breastfeeding made pregnancy weight come off quickly, there would be more naturally Barbie Doll-shaped women out there!

The saintly clerk at the maternity store told me that she nursed her babies for two years because she liked having big boobs. And, my saintly naturopath said she enjoyed having "big ta-ta's" for a while. I did not. I imagined, with horror, explosively large boobs for the entirety of breastfeeding. Thank God our milk production regulates and the leaking and swelling goes away. I think if it didn't there would be no pro-breastfeeding campaign in the universe that could convince women to breastfeed for years.

When I was engorged, I felt like the cartoon character that swallows a grenade which explodes in his stomach, only it was in my boobs. At full engorgement, my left boob was so painful I expected the skin to tear; it made my huge third-trimester belly seem elastic. It felt like when you've held your pee too long and it hurts your bladder to move, even to pee. My boobs would grow and grow until they could hold no more, and then squirt milk everywhere, including My Little Milkaholic's face. (He didn't seem to care.) Apparently, that's common. My saintly naturopath said she remembers when her nursling would fall asleep while nursing and slip off of her nipple, only to be awakened by milk squirting in his face.

I was shocked when I learned that another new mom I'd met – whose baby was a week older than My Little Milkaholic – wasn't leaking and didn't have to wear the weird boob-flattening leak pads only a month or two after her baby's birth.Though our bodies do settle into what our babies need, for at least six or seven months, every time My Little Milkaholic changed his sleeping/nursing patterns I would end up explosively, painfully engorged. Saint Riona, mother of the Hungry Hungry Hippo latcher, told me she started leaking when she was five months pregnant. "I was like, if I have any trouble feeding this baby, that will be totally unfair," she said.

The Best Husband Ever loved that I had big boobs, but it took until my milk regulated – about three or four months – before I would even let him touch them. They were too sensitive (not in the good way, but in the painful way) and I worried about milk exploding everywhere while we were having sex. Not sexy.

My Best Friend told me that when her breasts became seriously engorged at night, to that hard as a rock, hurts to move point, her "otherwise fairly indifferent [soon to be ex-] husband would get turned on and wanted to fondle my firm, very large breasts."

I can see why post-partum women sometimes kill their husbands.

As you probably know, the human body is not symmetrical. This was only magnified by my milk production. My huge breastfeeding boobs turned out to be one huge breastfeeding boob, and one low-flow boob. My left breast could swell to the size of My Little Milkaholic's three-month-sized head when engorged, while my low-flow breast looked only like a small water balloon. A hairdresser told me she didn't nurse more than a month or two because her boobs were so uneven she felt like a freak.

I read somewhere and heard stories in lactation group about feeding in particular boob order to fix the asymmetry, so I religiously fed My Little Milkaholic on the low-flow side first hoping to increase milk production on that side, to no avail! All the resources I looked at said starting with the low flow boob was supposed to work because babies suck more vigorously at first to stimulate let down. Unfortunately, I was so low-flow on that one side that My Little Milkaholic wouldn't keep his latch. He would suck for a few seconds and pop off, even after a month of religiously starting on the low-flow side. I knew he could get milk if he tried, but he just wouldn't do it.

Some women recommended doing one boob per feeding to give the low-flow boob time to produce milk. This only worked

[handwritten margin notes: "same here!!"; "left is smaller + leaky. right but big doesn't leak."]

at night when My Little Milkaholic would give me eight hours between feedings to get engorged, which was the only time that one boob had enough milk to feed him. Apparently this style of one boob feeding, called block feeding, is also good if you're evenly engorged and have a fast letdown that overwhelms your baby. I think it allows the baby to relax into one good boob rather than just have all rushing-river all-the-time feedings.

The blogs and lactation consultants also said to pump the low-flow boob after each feeding to stimulate the milk production more. That just sucked, both literally and figuratively. Nothing like getting My Little Milkaholic calm, and then having to forgo cuddling in order to attach myself to a cumbersome pump and continue to work my sore and tired nipples. So I didn't.

After a month of successful feeding in general, I switched to starting on the full side and finishing on the low-flow side. Once his desperation for milk subsided, he would calmly nurse, staying latched, for a longer period on the low-flow side. Since babies have more sucking power than a hospital-grade pump, I figured this approach had to be at least as good as pumping afterward, and kept me from getting frustrated, which is the best medicine for breastfeeding problems. While it didn't change the realities of my uneven production, it at least evened out the appearance by emptying my full boob and leaving some in my low-flow boob.

I used bra pads to absorb leaking milk until my body regulated and quit leaking (at about five months), and padded nursing bras, rather than shelf bras, to make my massively asymmetrical boobs look more normal. Some women suggest cleavage cupcakes for the smaller boob – AKA gel push-up inserts – to even out your look. My vanity sometimes falls more on the ridiculous side[21], so I eventually let go of any mutant-boob concerns.

But, not before I tried a padded bra and a shelf-bra tank top to elevate my milk crates.

I believe that in deciding to write this book, I may have invited the muses to bless me with *all* the wonders of breastfeeding, sort of a be-careful-what-you-wish-for situation. (Or more likely a temporary bout of vanity did me in.) But at three in the morning, when I awoke to joint and muscle pain from the neck to my toes, like I haven't felt since the last time I had the knock-down-drag-out flu, I wasn't feeling so blessed.

In retrospect, it started with a bruised-like feeling in my right breast, which I attributed to wearing an underwire bra. But, in my sleep-dazed state, I didn't really make the connection. I hoped it was a toxin-release from yoga, and feared it was the five-year flu (every five years I get one good flu to boost my anti-bodies and then I'm good again). I could barely get out of bed to feed My Little Milkaholic.

After a few more hours of sleep I dragged myself out of bed, drew a bath and consulted Dr. Google. He said that it was

---

21   I wore an arrow headband (as in, looks like I'd been shot in the head with an arrow) through most of elementary school; when girls were doing the big curled bangs, I went for a straight-up statements; and when colored socks and Keds were in, I mixed them all up and wore different colored socks and different colored Keds.

not likely a toxin-release from yoga, but suggested mastitis, an infection of the milk ducts! I was momentarily terrified that I might have to take antibiotics. I spent the year before I got pregnant fighting off a Candida infection, the result of taking antibiotics for six years of kids-ski-instructor-related sinus infections, and was finally back to a good balance. I was not about to disrupt my newfound equilibrium.

I had read about a woman who pumped for four hours straight to get her infected blockage out, but the thought of pumping for hours was not appealing to me, to say the least. Luckily, Dr. Google had some other ideas, and assured me that not all mastitis involved infections. The advice for a blocked duct – the bruised like feeling in my breast – was, "Heat. Rest. Empty the breast." For the flu symptoms, the mommy support pages recommended ibuprofen, too.

Luckily, after a few more hours and plenty of "Heat. Rest. Empty the breast," the majority of pain was gone, and by the next day only a small amount of residual breast pain existed. Turns out the padded bra/shelf-bra tank top combo had pinched my ducts and caused the problem. Stupid vanity!

Mastitis is a sort of "normal" problem of breastfeeding, the curse of having tons of milk to feed our nurslings. OBs, GPs and pediatricians all diagnose it and offer the relatively easy solution of antibiotics. Some mommy blogs and midwives recommend pumping till the clog and even infection comes out, which can be hours of hell.

Of the women I talked to over the course of writing this book, at least two thirds had mastitis at least once; many had it numerous times like Saint Elizabeth. She suffered months of torture before she ended up feeding her baby soy formula. He didn't like the taste of antibiotic milk and so refused to nurse. She couldn't pump enough anyway to bottle-feed him breast milk, and he puked up everything else she tried.

Mastitis was also part of the reason my cousin Saint Jane chose to exclusively pump.

I would push it to three-and-a-half, maybe four hours between pumping sessions and my breasts would be bursting, and so of course, my ducts got clogged and then infected. It took me awhile to figure this all out. By then I'd had mastitis four times.

It was horrible. I would be just writhing in pain, pumping through the pain, tears streaming down my face. Poor, Awesome Husband was beside himself. He would rub my back, cheer me through the really painful part—when I first started pumping was when it would hurt the most. He'd make me tea, and cue up my favorite shows. I watched all of *Buffy*[22] and the

---

22   Seriously, a must watch in the first three months of having a baby and breastfeeding.

Gilmore Girls while pumping during the first couple months—and, of course; he really took care of Baby Man more than I did in the early days because I was basically incapacitated with all this. So he didn't get any sleep because he was taking care of both of us. He was such a champ.

I figured out how to get rid of it without antibiotics after the first time. As soon as I'd feel a lump forming, I'd put the heating pad on it and massage it while pumping it more frequently (which of course only added to the hell I felt I was living). I definitely staved off a few more bouts of it after the fourth time, though. And the second, third and fourth times I had it, it went away after a couple days as long as I kept the heat to it and pumped a lot.

After all the trouble Saint Monica had with cracked nipples, she, too, had to endure mastitis a few times:

I went to a La Leche meeting with Peanut, feeling like a truck hit me, and showed them my left breast wondering if I had a plugged duct, or what. They took one look at the bright red, rock-hard skin and said,

"Go to the doctor!" It was mastitis, and I was put on antibiotics immediately. I was averse to medications while breastfeeding, but had to do it. And in a week, I was not in pain anymore.

When Peanut was three months old, I became engorged, had red swelling, and again felt like a truck had hit me. And, again, it took ten days of antibiotics to heal the mastitis. Repeat at five months and seven months. Every time I waited too long to go in, hoping it was just a plugged duct that I could massage/heat/pump away. It became such a familiar pain that I should have known it was major when Peanut would latch and when the milk let down I would feel a piercing pain shoot through my breast all the way through my torso to my back. But, instead of knowing it was mastitis, it seemed I was just resigned to the pain being part of feeding him.

Before My Little Milkaholic was born, my doula had recommended buying Lecithin for some probably totally awesome reason that totally did not compute when she recommended it. Even The Best Husband Ever had no idea what she had said. Later, I figured out it was to help prevent mastitis. Research estimates incidents of mastitis to occur in about ten to thirty-three percent of lactating women[23]. Perhaps hospitals should hand out Lecithin with Lanolin.

Mommas with low milk production have it really hard. But, low milk production is obviously a problem and one that has a number of solutions. Over-production of milk is like the curse of Midas. No one pities you, because milk is so precious that how could too much be bad? It doesn't seem like a real problem. But having too much milk can make nursing super painful if your baby pinches to manage the flow, not to mention the pain of engorgement and the risk of mastitis and blocked milk ducts. Even "good" breastfeeding circumstances, like ample supply can be a bitch.

---

23   Mastitis Causes and Management, Department of Child and Adolescent Health and Development, World Health Organization, Geneva, 2000. http://whqlibdoc.who.int/hq/2000/who_fch_cah_00.13.pdf

CHAPTER 9

Woman vs. The Cover – Nursing in Public

More than the bottle debate, there is a great debate about breastfeeding in public that, as with everything else about babies that people debate, is completely irrelevant. People with and without children love to judge women who feed babies in public – or those who don't. I really don't understand why. Who cares what a mom does with her baby as long as she's taking care of it? I think most women do whatever they want or need regardless of what people around them think.

One of My Little Milkaholic's step-grandmas didn't feed any of her three nurslings in public because they were so loud, slurping and talking while they fed. Saint Phiala, said her second baby got so distracted that it was really difficult to breastfeed in public at first, or even in the house, so she only nursed in her nursery or her bedroom. By the time her nursling was a year old they were so good at it she posted pictures of them nursing on Facebook in celebration of National Breastfeeding Week.

Saint Elizabeth was really uncomfortable with nursing in public. She refused to nurse in restrooms due to the gross factor. Who can blame her? With her first child the only place she would go was to Babies R Us because they have nursing lounges. "It really cut down on the shopping available to me," she said. She got over most of her aversion with subsequent children, only to have a janitor at their preschool strike up conversation with her while she was trying to get her youngest nursling latched. "I wanted to say, 'Really? You think I want to chat right now?'" On the upside, she now has much less aversion to chatting with women while nursing.

Another saintly friend from my birthing class was never comfortable breastfeeding in public or with anyone around. At mommy get-togethers, she bottle-fed her nursling, while the rest of us – with varying levels of comfort – nursed, eyeing each other as if playing nursing chicken, while awkwardly trying not to look at each other's boobs, even though you can't help but look at skin, and waiting for one or the other of us to admit it was totally awkward. (Or maybe that was just all in my head, and everyone else was fine.)

The first time My Little Milkaholic successfully breastfed in public was at our favorite local bar. Yes, I "had a baby in a bar," and yes, that Reese Witherspoon line from *Sweet Home Alabama* ran through my head the whole time. But, in Colorado, every bar must also serve food, so really it was totally a restaurant – with a bar feel. It's also legal to have kids in bars until 8 p.m. So whatever. Quit judging me.

Anyway, we were out with friends who had not yet had babies, and so as not to make them uncomfortable, and because I was a newbie at this whole breastfeeding thing – still uncoordinatedly using the training wheels (nipple shield) – I went to the bathroom, which had a great velvet, formerly-arm chair. It was very pleasant feeding My Little Milkaholic there – until someone knocked. I tried to stall so he could finish, but at that point, feedings could take at least half an hour (he was a very efficient now that he could latch, but was a very thorough eater).

The bar wasn't busy and had unisex bathrooms, but I hadn't thought it through when I went into the bathroom or when the other person was knocking. Eventually, I acquiesced and packed up and let the woman in, who apologized because she was just looking for her friend. I thought about going back in, but decided to rejoin our friends. I tried one more time with the cover. The husband of the couple agreed with the pro-breastfeeding chatter out there, saying that breastfeeding in public didn't bother him, but that he likes it when women use covers. If they don't, he said, it's hard not to look because his eyes are pulled toward skin. It is why women wear short shorts and low cut blouses and guys play Frisbee shirt-less, so we can't really blame him.

Being those new parents who delusionally still thought we were cool and could maintain our pre-existing lifestyle, we went out to eat a lot the first four months of My Little Milkaholic's life. (Actually, we still eat out all the time because we can each only be bothered to cook a couple days a week. That leaves two or three day a week when we need someone else to feed us.) So, I had to get used to feeding My Little Milkaholic in public. But, it was a hard-won battle.

Nursing-specific covers, as opposed to blankets, are all pimped out these days. There are ties to keep them up around your neck, plastic or metal bands to create a rigid hole to peek at your nursling, and terrycloth pockets for wiping off the baby and/or storing stuff. And yet, for some of us, using a cover requires practice. Somehow, it took me what seemed like forever to figure out how to get the cover over both of us and get My Little Milkaholic on my boob without getting the cover in his mouth. Then once I finally did, he discovered his arms and hands, and began pulling it off and waving it around like a flag announcing what we were doing. He liked to see what was going on.

Talking to my saintly RN friend made me feel like I am now in an awesome secret club, where we know things like: babies rip covers off after about three months of age. "A little arm just creeps up through the viewing hole and tears it away." (The club is called mommy hood.) With her second kid, she used a burp cloth and by the third she just didn't care.

By about six months (this seems to be a big transition point for both mommies and babies), the Travel Boppy became my best friend. My shyness mostly wore off, and I was more comfortable using blankets or feeding without a cover if I was wearing a nursing tank top that covered my still-fat belly.

My Cousin in Scotland never had a problem breast-feeding in public. "I think I found it totally possible to do it without any additional covers without anybody really noticing. Maybe because while breastfeeding, my breasts were massive!!"

Phiala said she's nursed her babies publicly everywhere – California, Kansas, Colorado, in restaurants, malls, outside, on airplanes – and never had any problems. "So, I'm always surprised to hear when women are given a hard time for public nursing," she said. "My father jokes that I'm like the French women because we just whip out our breasts. I've gotten a lot of support from my parents and husband. But, frankly, whether or not I had support, I still would have done it." One time, she was nursing her baby in the yard of her other daughter's camp (in Colorado), without a cover when another mom walked by, looked at her, and then turned around and gave her a thumbs-up and mouthed, "Good for you!"

New Mexico is quite supportive of breastfeeding, said Saint Adele, "So, many women just 'whip it out and go for it," she said. "I routinely see moms nursing without any covering or Hooter Hider. Moms feel comfortable here to nurse in public and it's widely accepted. I know a few years ago, New Mexico was in the top few states in the U.S. for percentage of breastfeeding moms."

Colorado legally protected the right of women to breastfeed in public in 2008. The Colorado Breastfeeding Coalition posted a flier in my favorite coffee shop, which surprised me, because I've never heard of anyone being denied service or being kicked out of anywhere for breastfeeding. I do have a kidless friend who got offended when a woman breastfed in public in D.C., but apparently it was more the scene the woman made that was offensive than the act of breastfeeding itself.

An awesome saintly author-friend had an embarrassing

public breastfeeding moment when she was breastfeeding at an outdoor performance by the Ballet Folklorico de Mexico. "My baby stopped nursing and pulled off my breast. I didn't notice until someone else pointed out that my boob was hanging out totally exposed. Fortuitously, about then all of the female ballet dancers came on stage topless and danced. I felt much better."

The funniest story I heard was from a well-seasoned pro. The Best Husband Ever's saintly college friend really didn't have any problems nursing either of her children (though her sleep stories are what nightmares are made of – or would be if she'd ever gotten any sleep). One day, shortly after she'd starting teaching belly dancing, she was hanging out in a Starbucks in the Mojave Desert when one of her students came in. The dance student went up to our friend and asked her to break down a hip articulation combination. With her nursling on the breast, under cover, she gave an impromptu dance lesson right there in the coffee shop. "[Nursing] was literally something I could multitask in almost any situation," she said. Talk about a great way to get her waistline back, nursing and dancing!

In the end, the great to-nurse-in-public or not-to-nurse-in-public debate comes down to what makes you and your baby happy.

CHAPTER 10

And Then There Were Teeth (Or the Beginning of Weaning)

For My Little Milkaholic's four-month birthday, he got a tooth, and I was obscenely happy about it. It was a tooth! I suppose it was the surprise, I hadn't thought about teeth at all. I couldn't stop showing it off and trying to get pictures of it. By about four and half months, he had two teeth – two bottom teeth, to be exact. To my great relief, my sweet baby did not bite. But, feeding him began to hurt again, especially at night.

After a couple of weeks, the pain was back up to a five. So like a good little breastfeeding student, I ran back to the lactation group ready to learn all sorts of new secret breastfeeding techniques, which I was convinced existed. Unfortunately, teething wasn't our problem, or so The Guru's LC-in-Training said. He needed to have his tongue-tie revisited, they said. The Guru guessed that it was still about forty percent tied.

I was not surprised, because I had convinced myself that tolerable pain was close enough. But, if I were to be honest with myself – which I had not been up to that point –breastfeeding had not ever been completely painless, I sat at a two or three on the pain scale most of the time. They said he couldn't get my milk out with full efficiency because his tongue was still not fully functioning. Which was why I was still making a ton of milk – so much, in fact, that I could squirt it into his mouth.[24]

It also explained my "E" cup and continued engorgement, as well as my continually squished and white nipples, which I pretended not to notice.

Knowing what to expect at the dentist, the visit for his second frenectomy, seemed to go faster (it was the same length of time) and be less bloody and painful (it was about the same). And within a week or so, breastfeeding really was mostly painless. My Little Milkaholic was sticking his tongue out, making zerberts (ppthtth) and, over the next couple months, mimicking most other tongue actions and noises I could come up with. For a while, sticking his tongue out was his favorite greeting. He would look around a busy room and stick his tongue out at anyone who looked at him or said, "Hi."

When I was pregnant and people asked how long I was going to breastfeed I answered flippantly, "A year, or until he bites me." Now, among the people who really know me, it is a well-known fact that my quips about my intentions or reasons for doing or not doing just about anything are often made completely of shit. Not on purpose, but as a protective mechanism, and because I'm clueless. So this response was met with a range of responses, from

---

24   The Guru says breast milk has great healing powers and should be used on cuts and scrapes and eye infections and all sorts of other ailments. This sounds suspiciously like "Windex" from My Big Fat Greek Wedding.

"Uh huh. Sure," to "Oh, ouch. They bite?"

After I had My Little Milkaholic and we got the breastfeeding thing down, I thought I might make it to eighteen months. I had been warned that breastfeeding to twenty-two months can become awkward. A saintly aunt told me of how her twenty-two-month-old once reached up under her shirt in public to feel if she had milk. That was the moment she decided it was time to wean.

At six months old, My Little Milkaholic cut his third and fourth teeth (two top front). It took him a few bites (met with involuntary swats to the diaper), to realize that these new teeth were sharp. However painful being bit on the nipple is (and it is a new level of pain), it felt mean to cut him off. After all, he was just learning about his teeth. Also, he was only six months old and I had no idea how else to feed him. We'd been giving him regular food, but I am way too lazy to mush it up or mix cereals. So we did baby-led weaning and just gave him whatever we were eating (that he could hold). It was a great, if somewhat inefficient, method for the first few months.

I remembered that in one of my first lactation groups a woman spoke about feeding her baby girl while healing from a bite-injured nipple. This is still one of the most amazing things to me (and another case-in-point of the shit we go through). The LC assured her (and us), that it is OK to reprimand our babies for biting. After all, they don't know it's painful. So, when My Little Milkaholic bit, I screamed, swatted and pulled my boob away. It worked. He went back to feeding like the sweet baby he was.

Then he got two more teeth, and my flippant response of "A year, or whenever he bites me," seemed distinctly realistic. My saintly stepmother, a nurse, told me "nursing strikes" – when babies quit nursing while teething – "were totally normal." Not for My Little Milkaholic; he wanted more milk and he wanted to soothe his sore gums on me!

After getting cut off a few times for biting, he started to learn. When he wanted to feel the pressure on his gums he would s-l-o-w-l-y pinch down with his whole mouth and lips until I warned him not to bite. If he got me unexpectedly, I'd sometimes scream and always put my boob away, which would make him cry since he was usually not done eating. When I jibed that he had no reason to cry, because I was the one who'd been bitten, he'd smile coyly at me and decide he wanted to go play.

While biting is awful, it was the squishing of my nipples that pushed me to decide I would wean him at a year. Once again, my squished, teethed-on nipples hurt with a sharp stinging pain, much like I imagine a pierced nipple might feel. This pain typically lasted for a few hours. Then, as the pain subsided, the tingling took over. This felt much like a limb going numb – the pins and needles feeling – with a sinking feeling that permanent damage had been done, again. His tongue was functioning just fine, but when he was really tired or cranky or needy, or all of the above because he was in pain from teething, he would use me like a pacifier. My nipples would come out flat and white, and would hurt the rest of the day. I took my calcium and B6 religiously, and burned through lanolin. But, I was sick of the pain. I wanted to cuddle My Little Milkaholic and soothe his emotional issues, not be his feeding machine/teething toy. Weaning seemed better for our relationship.

Because we are travelers and have family all over the country and were determined not to change our lifestyle any more than we had to, The Best Husband and I took My Little Milkaholic on three trips by the time he was eight months old. At five months, we paraded him around Las Vegas in a chest carrier to many *Hangover* associated high-fives and quotations. At six months, he was featured in his aunt's wedding (the one traumatized by my allergic nipples); and at seven and a half months his grandparents got to babysit him while we went to The Best Husband Ever's class reunion. Every time we came back from a trip, My Little Milkaholic came back with a couple more teeth. It was like they were his version of souvenirs.

On the flight home from the last trip, I could not soothe My Little Milkaholic. All he wanted to do was nurse, from 5 a.m. until well into the flight. Around 10 a.m., I just couldn't do it anymore. I wanted to cry. I don't know if I had any milk left, but he wouldn't stop nursing and wouldn't go to sleep. Desperate, I pulled out a bottle we'd brought for water and had the flight attendant fill it with milk. My Little Milkaholic chugged it and immediately fell asleep. It was another one of the most relieving moments for me in the first year of his life. Knowing I could feed him milk from somewhere else took so much pressure off me.

I continued to breastfeed him in our normal rhythm, but supplemented a bottle of whole cow's milk when we were in public or when he was teething and being extra needy. I immediately fell in love with cuddling My Little Milkaholic while he drank from a bottle. It was the relaxing, bonding time I had been promised, but had never really felt. While breastfeeding, I would get bored (I finally started playing Angry Birds), and because of the pain, I never relaxed. But with the bottle, he would nestle into me and I could kiss him as much as I wanted (which was kind of constantly).

By ten months, My Little Milkaholic had twelve teeth and showed no signs of taking a break from teething. Dr. Google said to pull out my nipple every time he bit to modify his behavior, but the problem wasn't biting. It was the constant squishing that hurt. I thought about going back to the lactation group, but never did because I didn't think they would have any new information for me. Having not said anything about techniques the last time, I didn't assume they would have any this time, either. Still, I was convinced there was some secret technique to breastfeeding that I did not know about. It turned out I was right, there are more techniques. I wish I had found out earlier, but at least I discovered I was right. (I mean who doesn't like being right?)

Finally, I reached out to my adorable saintly doula for another LC reference. The other Highly Recommended LC listened patiently to my long (but CliffNoted), story and had something new to say. First, she suggested going to an infant chiropractor.

She said that if My Little Milkaholic's jaw or neck were out of alignment it could cause the muscles to tighten, making him clench while feeding, thus squishing the heck out of me. Second, she said to beware of fast-flow bottles because they teach babies to chomp and squish when they eat to control the flow (though she did not tell me to stop using bottles). Of course, when I Googled slow-flow bottles, they didn't seem to exist. Finally, she said to try feeding him with his head tipped back and chin tipped forward, and to talk to him before feeding, showing him how to open his mouth big.

The Highly Recommended LC said babies are smart and will regulate the flow of milk on their own. This, however, is not always ideal for mommies, as it usually means clamping down painfully on our nipples. She recommends nursing with your newborn sitting up with their butt in your lap, leaning back a bit so that their head is above the boob. Gravity will help slow the flow. She also suggested a couple of other ways to slow the flow: compress the boob and feed your baby on your side, so that pressure from the bed slows the flow. Also, a nipple shield helps slow the flow until your body regulates the amount of milk your nursling needs.

At ten months, breaking habits is hard, she said, but My Little Milkaholic was old enough to reason with. On the first try, the new technique seemed to help. He got a full boob-latch and the pain, possibly from residual injury, was down to like, a three again. But, it took me awhile to figure out the positioning so that I was comfortable and not leaning forward over him. My Little

Milkaholic came out average sized, but he quickly grew to the one-hundredth percentile for height and sixtieth percentile for weight. He seemed too big for these new positions, and being a visual learner, I did not quite grasp them.

Bad habits seemed like as good of an explanation as any, especially given that My Little Milkaholic still had nursing callouses that were supposed to have gone away months before, and no one seemed to think teething caused nursing problems. But, I wanted to be sure nothing was really wrong, so we took My Little Milkaholic to the chiropractor that the Highly Recommended LC recommended. The chiropractor explained her process, examined My Little Milkaholic and extrapolated all the things that could be wrong. And then she sent us home, after charging us an arm and leg and not actually adjusting him. Unsettled, we decided she was not the chiropractor for us. I still was concerned about TMJ (the possible tight jaw), and the chiropractor saying that his neck was out of alignment. I suspect crashing as he learned to pull himself up onto the furniture caused his neck crick.

I found a second chiropractor who specialized in kids, didn't suggest weekly visits, was reasonably priced and was an expert in scoliosis[25]. She examined and adjusted My Little Milkaholic, confirming that his back was out, probably from running into things. She assured us that he was fine and was not in

---

25   Like any good hypochondriac, I chose My Little Milkaholic's doctors based on their ability to deal with the myriad issues that I could conceive of. It takes preventive medicine to a whole new level - his doctors could say they prevented a bunch of issues he never was going to get!

danger of developing TMJ, and said his jaw was not super-tight, though she could tell he was teething because he was clenching.

I thought about having the Highly Recommended LC come give me a tutorial, but since I was only planning on breastfeeding for another couple of months, I wasn't sure it was worth the cost. Because it was near the end of the year, we were almost out of insurance reimbursement funds, and I worried that if insurance didn't cover it outright, we would just end up paying for it.

For some reason, I expected weaning to be difficult, and worried about it for months before we were even thinking about it for real. That's probably because everything else was hard, and maybe because I assumed that if some women nurse their babies for years it as because their babies didn't want to stop. But, it's probably because I am not a procrastinator. Why put off to until tomorrow, what you can worry about today?

Just before we took My Little Milkaholic to the chiropractors, I warned The Best Husband Ever that I would decide when we weaned, and that I was going to make it at least a year. He told some of our friends something like exactly what I had said, that it wasn't worth spending the time or money to get My Little Milkaholic's bad habits fixed, since we were only planning on nursing for a year. Isn't he cute, listening to and repeating the logical things that I say? Of course, after trying to get more help, I decided (again) we would make it to eighteen months. It helped that nursing had become somewhat less painful due to a teething lull. The Best Husband Ever very smartly acquiesced to my wishy-washiness and gave me his support. Silently.

After being relieved of my fears that My Little Milkaholic's jaw was the reason for our nursing problems, we left on yet another trip, this time visiting friends and family in the Northwest. We had so much fun on our trip that I unintentionally quit breastfeeding My Little Milkaholic during the day and, sometimes, at night. When we were off schedule, or in public (he became really annoying to feed in public) or if I had a drink, we would give him a bottle of milk. He did not seem to mind at all. He slept through the night and was happy to nurse in the morning.

When we got home, he again grew more teeth and the painful breastfeeding came back. I could no longer deal. The first chiropractor had expressed amazement that I had lasted ten months with all my trouble and pain. That this was a feat rang in my head. Since My Little Milkaholic drank from a bottle like the Little Milkaholic that he is, I decided it was OK to quit breastfeeding. It seemed natural. He was busy exploring, and as long as he got milk from somewhere, it didn't seem to matter to him that it came from me.

Talking to my saintly Cousin in Scotland and a saint in New Zealand helped quell most of my feelings of failure and judgment. My Friend In New Zealand said:

Breastfeeding was uncomfortable - sometimes bordering on painful for me for the first six weeks. I remember thinking at four weeks, 'Right, that's it! I'm going to three months and that is absolute maximum.' Then at six weeks it just stopped being painful or uncomfortable, and after that it was pretty easy.

At four and a half months Doozle Bug fussed (not like him at all), at his 10 a.m. feeding, for three days; and on the third day, I just gave him a bottle of formula, which he gulped down. From that day forward, the 10 a.m. feeding was a bottle. I remember being super nervous about my four-month Plunket[26] appointment because we had started mixed-feeding. I told the nurse, and she just said, 'Oh, you did four months of breastfeeding? That's heaps and fine. Good on you.' She did not fuss at all that I was mixed-feeding.

Then a few weeks later, we did a morning and afternoon bottle and still breastfed other times, very gradually, until he was seven months old, at which time we totally stopped breastfeeding, which was both of our choices.

---

26   Plunkets are where "Infant-trained nurses visit you every couple of months to weigh your baby and check in to see how feeding is going and how you are doing. They also give you a lot of advice about how and when to introduce solids."

My Cousin in Scotland said when she offered her baby girl rice for the first time at four months old, her nursling grabbed the spoon and shoved it in her mouth herself. "The advice here is to not wean until six months, but I think she would have eaten her own hands by then." Her baby boy, on the other hand, was less interested in food until much later. He went from being a ten-pound newborn to the other end of the scale, and she got in trouble with the health visitor[27] because he was not putting on enough weight. "She told me to give him Angel Delight – not sure if you have that in the States. It is a sort of instant chocolate pudding that you whip up with milk. I decided that weaning a baby on chocolate wasn't such a good idea so I didn't do it." Despite crawling at five months, he did not really start eating properly until a year. He ate solids in small quantities, but was fussy. However, at the age of eight, he is a very good eater and "not really very fussy at all." Everyone weans and eats differently. I like the European idea that any amount of breastfeeding is a success, as compared to the American pressure to make it to a specific age.

For Saint Monica, the beginning of the end of breastfeeding came when Peanut was nine months old. She went on a road trip and didn't feel well, again:

> I thought I was having allergies because of sinus pain
> and sore throat, and didn't go to a doctor because we

27   Like a Plunket nurse.

were away from home. My energy decreased and my discomfort increased, and I was weak and depleted for five or six days before I went to the emergency room in rural Nebraska. They immediately diagnosed me with an ear infection, and I got on antibiotics, yet again. During this sickness, my milk supply dropped greatly as I was too tired and dehydrated to nurse sufficiently.

Then, a couple weeks later, I got my period for the first time in eighteen months, and I nursed less and less because less and less milk let down. I talked to a woman who got her period two months after the baby was born and was still breastfeeding fine at eight months, so I guess that getting my period wasn't actually a predictor.[28]

It has only been seven to ten days since we fully weaned, and I do miss it. Yes, I am going to miss that sweet time – experiencing the miracle and natural humanity of feeding my son with my body – but I am ready for my hormones to be regulated and looking

---

28   Despite medical rhetoric that it is hormones that cause menses to cease while breastfeeding, I think it is God's way of giving us time to forget the pain of contractions.

forward to some semblance of other parts of my identity resurfacing.

This experience has definitely taught me that with breastfeeding, nothing is normal. Despite all of the drama and pain, there were pleasant times and loving bonding occurred throughout all of it. And my son got plenty to eat through the whole process, which is absolutely a miracle to me when I think about all of the stumbling blocks that could have easily caused me to quit. I feel so lucky that I was able to work at home this first year of his life. So, the seemingly constant adversity was also less likely to deter me because I could deal with it in the privacy of my home. This has been so therapeutic to document.

Saint Phiala said she nursed her first baby for three years. Her daughter was, and still is, the kind of kid that prefers to know things ahead of time, so about three months before she turned three, Phiala would tell her nursling – over and over – that when she turned three, "No more milky." Her nursling would repeat it with her with a smile. She was totally OK with weaning by the time she turned three and Phiala quit breastfeeding her.

It took six months for Phiala's milk to go away after weaning her first baby. My saintly stepmom's milk continued for a year, which is probably because my little brother stopped nursing suddenly at five months, despite her healthy milk production. My milk seemed to disappear quickly, but it took two months for my nipples to turn from purple back to their normal red/pink color, and the tips to turn from white and cracked-looking back to normal. I was relieved that they did heal, and that no permanent damage seems to have been done. Although, when it gets cold, they do turn a vibrant shade of purple again.

My name is Cassi Clark, and I breastfed My Little Milkaholic for only ten and a half months. I say this in an AA confessional tone, because it felt like failure. But let me tell you (and myself), right here and now, it is not. Anyone who attempts breastfeeding for any length of time is a champion, and don't let anyone (especially that bitch in your head), tell you otherwise! Breastfeeding. Is. Hard.

CHAPTER 11

The Bottle Battle

When I started breastfeeding, I had no idea that using bottles was controversial, a positive side effect of not doing research. My Little Milkaholic thrived in his first month because of bottles; he and the Best Husband Ever bonded early because of bottles; my nipples healed because of bottles; and The Best Husband Ever and I got to go on dates because of bottles.

A saintly PA friend of ours did her due diligence and went to a breastfeeding class before she had her baby. She found the class to be enlightening, providing her with beneficial information. In the class, the teacher encouraged breast-only feeding to avoid nipple confusion. "This makes sense unless you have issues with getting a good latch," our friend said. "There was not enough emphasis on what to do if you had latching issues. It is after you have issues, that everyone comes out and admits how much breastfeeding can suck."

As is often the case, my friend had huge milk-filled boobs and a tiny baby. "I was doing everything right, her latch looked good, though I was in a lot of pain," she said. Her baby also fell asleep at the breast. (I wonder if that isn't caused by getting a lot of milk really quickly and being full enough to sleep, or perhaps from being wiped out from working hard at a bad latch.) Either way, her pain only worsened despite assurances that everything was fine and that the pain was normal. She eventually ended up with cracked and bloody nipples as well. Luckily, our PA friend is a smart girl and dragged her four-day postpartum self (and baby), to a lactation group, where she was told to pump and use a bottle until her nipples healed. "I still had this internal desire to only breastfeed, but in the end, the goal was for my nursling to gain weight appropriately via breast or bottle. We never had issues with nipple confusion, and she went back to breastfeeding just fine. And, once she was over eight pounds, her latch was good, and my nipples were healed."

In the first month of her nursling's life, my insanely-saintly PA friend came down with pneumonia. "Thank goodness we had introduced the bottle early, as I was then able to spend fifteen minutes pumping, and then have my husband give my nursling a bottle at night instead of me struggling with her then one-hour-long-feedings." Turns out, sleep deprivation from feeding every three hours is not good for any kind of recovery, and bottles are not the worst thing ever.

She also reported that her pediatrician shared studies with them that show that women who supplement with formula end up breastfeeding longer.[29] "Probably because all that pressure is off to just give breast milk," she smartly suggested. And, a friend of hers in Australia said that it is common for women there to never introduce bottles because they get a full year of maternity leave. As a result, women who don't use bottles at all can't go out on date night or momma's night out because they must always be available to nurse. I'm a big supporter of six months to a year maternity leave, but six months without a full night's sleep, and a year without a date night or bottle of wine might be more than I could personally deal with.

Bottles are a funny topic in the breastfeeding world. For women who easily slide into breastfeeding, bottles do not seem to be an issue. Either they don't use them, because they don't need to, or they do use bottles when they go to work or are away from their babies. But either way, it's not a big deal. But for women with breastfeeding problems, bottles are like God on the dollar bill – if you buy into the rhetoric, they are evil and will harm your baby. But, once you really use them, you see that they are generally very useful, and while they can sometimes be troublesome, they are

---

29   I don't have the exact studies our PA friend's pediatrician referenced, but one small study conducted by Dr. Valerie Flaherman, an assistant professor ofpediatrics and epidemiology and biostatistics at the University of California, San Francisco in 2013 found that "after three months, 79 percent of the babies in the study who received early limited formula in the first days of life were still breastfeeding, compared with 42 percent of the babies who did not receive early limited formula. Additionally, 95 percent of the babies who received limited formula in the first few days were breastfeeding to some extent at three months, compared with 68 percent of the babies who did not receive early limited formula." http://www.ucsf.edu/news/2013/05/105831/early-formula-use-helps-some-mothers-breastfeed-longer

rarely as troublesome as represented.

In modern baby feeding, our lives are ruled by ounces. First, it is how many ounces is he or she gaining? Then, how many am I pumping? How many is he or she eating? Since the invention of bottles (which was in the Stone Age – literally[30]), and breast pumps (invented sometime post stone age), we know more about how much our nurslings eat, and that makes us feel comfortable. Bottle-feeding allows for control. The nice little marks on bottles allow us to track our baby's exact intake, which is nice since boobs do not come with such nifty measurements.

Our saintly friend from birthing class, with nipples made for nursing, said that even though breastfeeding went fairly smoothly, she still got insecure and apprehensive. She worried about whether or not she produced enough milk, if her milk had too much foremilk and gave her nursling gas, and if he fussed because of the food she ate, etc. "I think with formula things are a bit more straightforward," she said. When her husband introduced the bottle to her nursling, she watched with uneasiness, almost jealousy, as if her nursling was losing his bond with her. "So silly because it was my milk. But when I fed him, it was a special moment that we got to share between us." That desire to bond during feedings is so strong! As I said before, my favorite time with My Little Milkaholic was when he cuddled with me and drank his bottle – stress free for both of us.

---

30   Suzanne Barston wrote a book that probes the politics of breastfeeding, and shares archeological findings of a four-thousand-year-old bottle. *Bottled Up: How the Way We Feed Babies has Come to Define Motherhood, and Why it Shouldn't*

From the source is usually best, and doctors try to help us with time measurements (based on some unknown rate of flow that I cannot believe every women lactates at), and LCs help us to know how much our babies eat by weighing them before and after feedings to confirm appropriate gains. But, if a momma is having trouble producing enough milk or getting her nursling to latch, supplementing with a bottle can be a lifesaver and a stress-reliever.

It never occurred to me to not give My Little Milkaholic a bottle, maybe because of the dehydration event in the beginning. But, one of the side effects of a month of bottle-feeding was hyper awareness of how much he ate. While still trying to get him to breastfeed, I would guess how much he was getting from me based on how much of a bottle he would take afterwards. The flaw in my method was that My Little Milkaholic would (and still does a year later) drink as much milk as we give him. (At a year old, our pediatrician suggested that maybe a half gallon of milk a day was not necessary – he'd jumped to the eightieth percentile in weight.)

Generally, My Little Milkaholic can really hold his milk. He didn't spit up, he didn't puke, he really didn't even let much milk dribble out once it hit his mouth. But periodically, he would regurgitate two to four ounces back on me – somehow not on my mother-in-law, or The Best Husband Ever – just me. It was not the cute little spit up that we bought the requisite burp cloths for. It was the milk we had just filled him with, in the same form as it went in, coming back all over me like a popped water balloon.

We started with Dr. Brown's bottles because Saint Saeran diligently researched products for her baby and then handed them down to us. We added a curved Aventi to our bottle repertoire, because that was the favorite of The Guru. When we switched to cow's milk, My Little Milkaholic chugged it from basic Evenflow jewel-colored straight bottles. He was never confused[31].

In New Zealand, they really push breastfeeding (a government directive), so much so that they won't even teach bottle-feeding. But, my saintly friend who lives there has a good outlook. She said:

> One of the girls in my class never wanted to breastfeed, and bottle-fed by choice from the get-go, but she had to be 'pushy' to do this.

I honestly see nothing wrong with formula feeding. Actually, when a friend of mine's son was two weeks old, she was in absolute agony, and it wasn't doing

---

31   Dr. Mom, Marianne Neifert, MD, MTS, FAAP, clarifies that the phenomenon known as "nipple confusion" is an exaggerated fear that came from situations where milk wasn't being stimulated because a baby wasn't suckling enough, presumably because of over bottle feeding. However, she says, "troubled breastfeeding, calls for special measures." And that pumping can help mitigate low supply/stimulation issues. (http://www.dr-mom.com/blog/breastfeeding-myths/) I briefly met a woman at The Guru's lactation class whose year+ old nursling preferred the bottle to her momma. But the two came to class and worked on techniques to get her nursling to latch, and it worked. She got a full fifteen-minute boob feeding right there with us, and said she was getting more and more nursing time at home.

her or her son any favours. She had an awful midwife who just kept telling her to 'harden up,' basically, and deal with the pain. Her husband went to the store and took pictures of tins of formula and sent them to me until I told him the one that we had used. She still breastfeeds a bit, but her son is mostly formula-fed, and she and her baby are much, much happier. Absolutely nothing wrong with it. I truly believe that whatever makes you and your baby the happiest (as long as they are getting enough to eat), is the best option for everyone. We put a number on nursing as if how long matters. It doesn't. In New Zealand new moms receive mega support, but if a mom stops at three months they call it a success."

The Highly Recommended LC told me that bottles flow too fast ("because the makers are in cahoots with formula companies who want our babies to drink more, so we buy more") and that bottle-feeding can teach babies bad habits like pinching our nipples or even biting. While that may have caused some of my issues later on, she did not try to suggest that using bottles was forbidden. Likewise, The Guru had me use the bottle to teach My Little Milkaholic to push his tongue out and feed with it rather than with his lips after he finally latched. Like anything, there are positives and negatives to bottles, and applying any one opinion to every situation is stupid. Do what works for you.

We often compare our ideas of what we should be able to do as modern pregnant or breastfeeding moms to tribal or imagined bygone women working the fields. The confidence and relief that bottles give us is probably why we are "culturally a bottle-feeding world" to the lament of lactivists everywhere. The delusion that "natural" means that somewhere there are entire cultures of women who don't have breastfeeding problems or use aids is silly and incorrect. It is important to remember that tribal women and our female ancestors relied on each other and bottle-like devices to feed their babies when breastfeeding was troublesome. Today we use electronic pumps and formula. Perhaps if we took this "it's natural (and therefore easy)" BS out of our conversations about breastfeeding, maybe more women would feel safe enough to push through the hard times with the use of nipple shields, bottles, pumps, formula, etc. – and without shame.

CHAPTER 12

So, Why Do We Do This?!?

Difficult breastfeeding is the most painful thing ever. Birth hurts, but like any good trauma, it can be buried deep in your psyche to be forgotten until you face it again (or see pregnant women on the street and suddenly feel the need to throw up for no identifiable reason.) But, difficult breastfeeding is like being kicked when you're down – in the boobs, which are raw nerve endings filled to exploding with milk.

A friend asked why I was so determined to breastfeed given all the troubles I had. I thought about my protective answers: pumping seemed worse; it's just what you do; people in the know recommend it; since it's natural, I was supposed to be able to do it. But, that wasn't it. I really didn't have an answer for her. Science tells us breast is best and we believe it. There isn't any indication that it isn't. And culturally, we are returning to breastfeeding after an era of germ concerns and an industrialization push towards formula. Science and culture may be why we try it. But the reason we stick with it is far more personal.

Saint Adele shared her personal motivation. She, like me I realized, was at some level motivated by pride. She wanted to and truly believed that she could breastfeed her baby, and told herself, "Women have done this for years, so why can't I?" She was against interventions like the nipple shield because she felt like they would take away from her experience as a first-time mom. "Somehow in my mind, I had told myself that those things were used by mothers who gave up on breastfeeding too early or didn't even try at all, and only wanted the 'easy' way out," she said. "Those thoughts were simply things that I made up because I was scared, tired and lost when things didn't go as planned. I feel like I have a completely new respect for the motherhood journey."

My pride was a motivator because I have never been one who accepts it when I'm told I can't do something. A seventh grade math teacher once told me I couldn't do algebra because I couldn't multiply. So I skipped eighth grade math and went all the way to calculus. When I get it in my head that I can do something, pretty much nothing can stop me. So it was with having a vaginal breech birth, and so it was with breastfeeding.

Fiachra, our friend's Irish saint of a mom, generously opened up and said that she had had a very disconnected relationship with her mother, and that all of her mothering decisions stemmed from that. "I desperately wanted the close mother-child bond with my children that I did not have with my own mother. I had no idea why [breastfeeding] was so important [at the time], but it was do-or-die for me. Bottles weren't even a back-up plan! I had no idea what I'd do if breastfeeding didn't work." And it wasn't just bottles. Fiachra wouldn't let her first baby use pacifiers, blankies, thumbs or anything to soothe herself that was not mommy. "It was extreme," she said. "And I have no problem telling you that in a couple of years I was in serious therapy." But, by the time she had her third child, Fiachra was using bottles judiciously on long car rides, and she weaned her second child to a bottle for his last feeding at night to put him to sleep. "By the end of this process I remember thinking, 'Wow, these bottles are so great!'" And to this day, she has great relationships with all her children.

After hearing her story, it occurred to me that I let My Little Milkaholic soothe himself on me, if not intentionally. By nine months (and eleven or twelve teeth), he stopped using a pacifier and only stuck his fingers in his mouth for his last few teeth. He didn't develop a favorite blanket or stuffed animal until after we weaned. I wish someone had pointed that out along my journey – validated my teething-is-painful-for-both-of-us theory – but figuring that out now may be more cathartic than in the moment. But it still didn't explain why I stuck with it. I wasn't intentionally being a good mom and letting him sooth on me, all I knew while I was in it, was the pain.

Saint Riona gets really mad at me when I call myself a bad mom. She thinks I'm putting myself down, but I'm really protecting myself from judgment – other people's and my own. You can't bully someone who beats you to it. Since I didn't find breastfeeding amazing, or all angels and rainbows, I felt I was failing as a mother. I think my obsessive motivation came from an idea in my head that a good mom bonds with her baby while breastfeeding. Since both the bonding and the breastfeeding came slowly for me, not to mention the mommy-identity, I felt that I had to get to a place where breastfeeding was blissful to prove to myself that I could be a good mom. Turns out, I needed to come to grips with my new identity, which I now love, to realize I'm an OK mom.

I was able to let go of my need to breastfeed when I realized that My Little Milkaholic and I bonded just as well while he drank his milk from any container he could get it out of, and that I loved that time and him. In the end, despite all the stress, pain and trouble, I am proud that I attempted breastfeeding. It gave me a project (this book) that I hope will help you and other new mommies, as well as helped me mix my pre- and post- baby identities, and breastfeeding was a challenge I survived. I am now a member of a club with very peculiar conversations and have tidbits and stories that freak out friends unfamiliar, which is always fun.

Breastfeeding is hard. It always has been. So cut yourself some slack.

Smart people say that when you have a baby, he or she should sleep where everyone gets the most sleep. This is good advice, and I say the same idea goes for breastfeeding. Feed your baby however you need to, so that your family gets the peace and bonding that you need. It is about you and your baby, so do what works best for you.

Let me just say, I don't think anyone has it truly easy, and no one who is feeding their baby is doing it wrong! Don't let the voices out there (and in your head), rule your experience. There is a lot of help out there, and many LCs will do it for free if cost or inadequate insurance is prohibitive.

Whether or not we breastfeed, and for how long, does not reflect how much we love our children. For some of us, the pain and frustration of breastfeeding hinders us from bonding with our babies. If anything, the time we make ourselves spend in agony and tear-jerking pain proves our willingness to do just about anything for our little ones – but is a torture we need not endure. Regardless, we deserve sainthood, or at least a second holiday.

So, go hug a nursing mom – but not too hard. Her boobs may hurt.

Made in the USA
Lexington, KY
22 April 2015